The Other Side of Normal

A survival guide for living in the intuitive age

Bonni McCliss

The **Other Side** of Normal

A Survival Guide for Living in the Intuitive Age

Bonni McCliss

www.psychicbonni.com

4465 Hwy 47 N

Charlotte TN 37036

Cover Design by Julia Singh

Interior Design by Bri Clark/Belle Consulting

ISBN 13: 9780999331002

Disclaimers

Fair use and library exemptions: Readers are encouraged and permitted to share this information with others or to incorporate portions into new works, under the condition that all such uses are solely with attribution and notice of copyright to this author, and within the fair use or library exemptions of the copyright law of the United Sates (title 17, United States Code), which governs the making of photocopies or other reproductions of copyrighted material. Anyone making a photocopy or reproduction (by any means) for purposes more than fair use without specific prior permission of the author may be liable for copyright infringement.

If you want to hear about all the wonderful upcoming happening from Bonni please sign-up for her email list here

Table of Contents

Dedication

With a heart full of deep gratitude and love I dedicate this book to my husband who has always shown me unconditional love and support and to Frances, the first person to see my gift and set me on my spiritual paths

Foreword

It isn't often in life that an event shakes your foundation so intensely that you doubt you will ever be able to function again. In the summer of 2016, in the early evening, my twenty-five-year-old daughter, Kristen was floating the Buffalo River and the canoe flipped over. Kristen didn't resurface and it took rescuers several hours to find and recover her body. I was on vacation and my older daughter, Kayce, called me at 2:00 a.m. with the news. Life as I knew it would never be the same. I would never be the same. How could I possibly go on?

It isn't by chance that I met Bonni McCliss. I sincerely believe that destiny and a higher power brought us together. She has walked with me through the most difficult leg of my journey, down a path no parent should ever have to travel. Combined with her beautiful gift and her compassionate soul, she is a big part of why I am not curled up in a ball in the corner of a room refusing to function any longer on this journey called life.

Bonni breaks the stereotypical mold of how most people in today's society view psychic mediums. Within minutes of being in her presence, it is obvious to all she touches that God chose her to deliver messages from the other side and she does so with compassion and love. Bonni's bubbly, vivacious personality puts people at ease, and a connection is made with loved ones on the other side which she delivers in a beautiful way. Her words are props for fallen hearts that bring needed assurance that our departed loved ones are never far away and are at peace.

If you often feel discouraged, not sure where you should be at this leg of your journey, and in need of guidance from a loving, caring soul, take a deep breath, flip the page and see what lies on *The Other Side of Normal.*

Karla Shepard

Chapter 1

Growing up Gifted: A Blessing and a Curse

Uncharted Beginnings

The beginning was beautiful. I was powered by wonder and mystery and the happy resident of two worlds. My earliest childhood memories, was a mystery ballet of beautiful pearlescent light that would hover over my bed at night and speak in a quiet language that only I seemed to understand. These dancing lights were incredible and interesting to me as a child. They seemed to communicate volumes without the use of any words. I felt as if they were a second mother, joyful and protective.

I remember looking forward to going to bed as a little girl—eager to watch the light show. Several times, I asked my mother about the lights above my bed. She would reassure me that I was safe, and that it was all in my dreams. I remember the hot topic of many of my nightly prayers to God was "How can I possibly be dreaming when I am wide awake"!

Reflecting back to these experiences, I now know that the lights were messengers helping to prepare me for what was to lay ahead—access to the other side of the veil.

I was a quiet little girl, naturally good at behaving yet still finding myself in constant trouble. My mother often seemed frazzled with my over active "imagination" and many invisible spirit friends. There is a running joke in my family about how I was kicked out of preschool as a final straw when I pushed a little boy from a chair insisting that he sat right on top of my invisible friend "Emily." My mother did her best with this uncharted child of hers, even going so far as to make dolls on her sewing machine to embody my imaginary friends. It didn't work—the spirits kept coming.

Fire in the Walls

One day when I was around 5 years old, I was sitting on my beloved strawberry Shortcake bed with my kingdoms of stuffed animals, as the spirit of an old woman walked through the wall and entered my room. She was not like the others; she scared me. The woman was dressed in black, angry and frantic. She kept pointing to the wall next to me. She made me understand that I needed to get immediate help. I went over to the wall and touched it. Strangely, it was hot.

The woman kept yelling; I felt paralyzed. I finally gained enough courage to run past her and out of my room.

My mother was taking her daily nap, I remember being conflicted to wake her (she did not react well when I would disturb her naps). I decided to tap her and tell her just that the wall was hot and not about the scary woman. It took some convincing for her to come and check the wall—I'm sure this was due to my reputation as a storyteller. My frustrated mother finally agreed to leave her nap and come feel the wall of my bedroom. I'll never forget her expression when she placed her hand on the wall—her eyes became wide and alert, as all the color drained from her face. In less than a second my mother turned on a dime, grabbed me and ran out of my room into the bathroom where we found the old wall heater on fire.

I remember hearing the firemen tell my mother how lucky we were, and that the old faulty wiring of the wall heater was what had started the fire burning inside of our wall. He told her that if it had not been found as quickly as it had, the fire could have taken out the whole house.

As I look back, I shudder to think what might have happened to an inattentive child and her deep sleeping mother without the visit of the old woman and her message of danger.

I never saw the old woman again. This event seemed to be a turning point in my world. One may think that such a scary experience would snap my head out of the clouds and cause me to become more attentive to my Earthy reality, however it did just the opposite. This event and the fear that it drew up only drove me closer into the protective bubble of the other side, allowing me to travel further down the rabbit hole.

First Glance at a Second Sight

Have you ever experienced someone questioning something that you never even once second-guessed as a normal part of life? It's like moving to the south from the west coast and everyone looking at you like you have two heads because you sound like you are from another planet. This was my experience of communication between worlds. I didn't think anything was "wrong" or "weird" as a child. This is how I came in to the world and everyone knows God doesn't make mistakes. I felt perfectly normal.

These spirit friends of mine often came and went. The more I became involved with "real" children my spirit friends seemed to take a back seat. Real children were the true phenomenon to me. They were fickle and sometimes even hurtful. There definitely wasn't the one-way street when it came to choose which game to play. We had to take turns and manage the relationship or it turned into hurt feelings resulting in lonely recesses. I gravitated towards the kids that had vivid imaginations; like Jennifer who told me that she was really a talking dog that shape shifted into child flesh during school hours. This made more sense to me than the average he said/she said playground drama.

As my school years progressed, more lines were drawn in the sand. It was becoming unanimous—that I was not "normal." I still remember the chants sung at the game "Red Rover," a game where two lines would form like a rope less tug-o-war, and children would chant and call their friends to the other side. "Red rover, red rover send freaky Bonni on over." I didn't mind the freak part, I was just praying they would call me and not leave me to be the last man standing.

The funny thing is, that it wasn't my ability to see and speak to the dead that isolated me from the other kids as much as it was my ability to know what they were feeling and thinking, and of course the even higher annoyance—my imagination. This was a deal breaker for the average fifth graders. They didn't want to explore their feelings, and they certainly didn't want to join me in a make-believe game about a magical dog who shape shifted into a human child.

More Than Words

One of my strongest gifts as a child was the ability to feel in great depth what other people were feeling. I know now as an adult this is understood as being "empathic." Feeling the emotions of others seemed to happen without my prompt or permission, I was just a walking magnet for emotional wavelengths. Somehow, I got it into my head that this was the same as allergies. I thought that if I sneezed I could release whatever seemed to me targeting me and causing my allergic reaction. I have no doubt that inducing sneezing by sniffing pepper to avoid heavy emotions added to my list of glaring oddities.

One day when I was around 11 years old, my mother took my little brother and me to a local diner. Once we were seated at our table, waves of strong emotions covered my whole body like fleas on a junkyard dog. I felt more sadness that I had ever experienced in all my 11 years. With every cell in my body I was drawn to look over to the man sitting alone staring in to space at the table next to us. I didn't want to live, and I had a bizarre thought of missing my wife. I was startled and confused at the rapidly unfolding experience. I recall the struggle I felt as my own emotions battled with those of a stranger. I burst in to tears, as my mother looked at me with her "what now" face. I told her that I thought the man was sad and lonely, and that I felt that we should join him for dinner because he missed his wife and he should not be eating alone. My mother studied the old man for a moment, and then explained that she thought the old man looked so peaceful, and that two loud children would most likely interrupt his peaceful dinner.

I could not eat that night or even the next day. I will never forget what it feels like to feel that kind of loss of a loved one. One of my biggest unanswered childhood questions was how that night my mother could see the old man as peaceful, when I felt him at his darkest hour.

Diagnosed Psychic

Things in this world are not always what

they seem. Sometimes what you think is the most important thing in life doesn't amount to much in the end, and the opposite holds the same truth. I used to think fitting in was the top priority. I tried. I really did. I remember the day I stopped trying. I was accustomed to seeing doctors and psychiatrists over the course of my life, but things changed when I arrived at my early teenage years. What was once considered childhood imagination, was now looking to adults as a serious mental and emotional condition. My childhood "imaginary friends" and other eccentricities were now a grave family problem. I was told by doctors that I was hallucinating, and that I had a condition called Schizophrenia.

I fought to keep my worlds separate my whole life until one day I became tired of fighting and agreed that I must be defective. I was put on heavy anti-psychotic drugs and fell into a deep depression. My visions and imaginary friends became distorted on the heavy drugs. I would often see men in bowler hats and black suits standing in my room watching me as I tried to fall asleep.

One night I remember being terrified as I experienced hallucinations of rats with red glowing eyes, coming out from under my bed, in fleets covering my bedroom floor, and scratching to climb up my bedside. My once enchanted world and beloved spirit friends had turned into a version of a dark cavernous hell in the matter of a few weeks. Most nights I spent lying on the floor crying in the hallway with my cheek pressed against my mother's bedroom door. I was afraid to upset my mother more than I already had.

I held the fright and paranoia to myself.

My depression took me even deeper and the doctor continued to increase and add more medication. I don't remember much after those weeks until I was told that I needed to be admitted to a psychiatric hospital. My first day was one of the most horrific things I had encountered to date. Upon my arrival of the hospital the nurses searched my belongings removing anything semi sharp and confiscated my shoelaces.

This was not one of the modern hospitals that is more common today. This facility was fully equipped with straightjackets and padded rooms. My only request was that I could keep my cassette player and my request was denied. The hospital staff explained that I could work up to having one as a privilege with good behavior. I felt like I was in a prison for crimes I didn't commit, with no one who would believe in my innocence. Terrible things happened in this hospital, it was like a real-life Twilight Zone. My roommate was removed due to claims of rape. I never saw her return. I watched as they placed out of control girls in padded rooms as they screamed their self to sleep. My medication was so high at one point I lost the ability to see. Everything was blurry and I could not continue the hospital's school.

I sat in corners and behaved my way to the promised privileges.

I earned the treat of having a watch. My mother brought me her beloved red-strapped Mickey Mouse watch, which I used to hold up to my ear throughout the day. The ticking helped me to stay sane.

I even earned my cassette player and listened to the Carpenters sing about birds and other beautiful things.

I was eventually found to be stable enough to return home, and was discharged with a rolodex of prescriptions. Months passed and all I did was lie in my mother's bed transfixed on her ceiling fan. My mother who I know tried to do what she felt was in my best interest, decided that it would be a good idea to put me in a private school, to help me re-enter the real world. She found a somewhat remote private Christian school, and enrolled me the following school year. Things had stabilized somewhat. The medication was finally not causing horrible hallucinations, and my contact to the other side was completely silent.

I was normal.

There was no way to predict the coming events that would follow me on my path to my new normal.

My new school was compromised of several freestanding trailers, along with a small administrative building. I was scared to enter this new school, but then again, most things scared me these days. My mother dropped me off as I overheard her telling my teacher about my prior situations. One of the other hardships we were facing was an abusive ex-husband that had become violent on many occasions. My mother had a court ordered restraining order against him. She told my teachers that under no circumstances were they to disclose my location to anyone but her, and if her ex-husband did show up, they needed to call the police immediately.

The trailer door closed and my mother drove away. My teacher was loving and had a beautiful smile as she asked me to find my seat. I was introduced to the class. My timidity must have been glaring, because the teacher reassured me that I was going to be happy in my new family. The next event that transpired was a true living nightmare. My teacher asked the class to bow their heads and pray. She led us all in a morning prayer ending it with "if it is your will God for us to be killed by Bonni's father, then we open our arms to the chance to return home to the promised land, and will feel blessed for this early departure. Amen"

It may sound crazy that I didn't bolt from the tiny trailer at that moment. I instead sat perfectly still. Although the statement scared me and made my blood run cold, I didn't see it as horrifying as the hospital I had left behind. I learned at the hospital that compliant behavior was rewarded. I didn't say a word, I just remember being embarrassed by the statement and squeezing my eyes tight pretending to be deep in prolonged prayer.

I didn't tell my mother what the teacher had said that day. I was still afraid to add more to her already painful life circumstances. In the coming weeks, the school didn't teach much that I can remember. We were just shown movies everyday about something called "The Mark of The Beast." This series of movies depicted different aspects from the "Book of Revelations," and the end of the world. One day a particular scene in one of the movies seemed to bother me more than usual. It was the scene showing barcoding and microchips in people's flesh that really upset me and I began to cry. The teacher's assistant pulled me into another classroom and was very kind as she inquired about the nature of my tears. I was too afraid to tell her that the movie scared me, in fear that they would think I was abnormal and not fitting in.

I still wanted so badly to make people happy.

Instead, I told the teacher about my

problems. I explained my trauma related to the hospital, and the medicine that I was on. I left out the part about once having friends that no one else could see. She treated me so kindly as she compassionately began to explain that she knew why I was having so many problems. She told me I was sick because the devil was living inside of me, and that they needed to do something to help remove the devil from my spirit. The woman went on to explain that the medication that I was taking kept the devil inside and that I needed to never take any of those pills again. She made me promise I would stop, and I agreed.

I felt more ashamed than ever. I believed that the devil had moved inside and found permanent residence. I was returned to my class just as we were all going outside to recess. I asked to use the bathroom and was granted permission. I headed toward the restroom and broke out into a run. I ran and ran, without ever looking back. I took refuge at the house of a nice older couple. They fed me, and told me stories. I calmed myself with the old man as he showed me how to bead safety pins together to make tiny Indian headdresses. I held their little white poodle in my lap, as I listened to them gently persuade me to call my mother so she knew where I was.

Some would ask where my guides have been through all the suffering and fear I encountered. I would tell them that I found my angels that day in the form of a little old man and woman. When I reunited with my mother I told her everything that the school had said and done. I remember her great upset and telling me that the school must be some sort of a cult. She never made me go back. I found out years later that the school was closed for cult practices.

My life experiences had broken my beautiful.

I no longer felt any connection to the light that once guided me. I refused to take any more medication after I was told it was the cause of the devil inside, and still I seemed to lost, and unfocused. Years passed and I maintained my life with the belief that I was still a closet schizophrenic. I eventually hit critical mass with my anxiety reaching an all-time high and was having thoughts of not wanting to live. I returned to therapeutic sessions, despite my fear of doctors and being committed to a mental hospital once again.

The woman I was set up to see, was heaven's intervention. I cried and bared my soul in the first session. I felt compelled to tell her my whole story, leaving no stone unturned. She sat quietly and listened. I could feel light as I use to know it radiating from her sweet spirit. The following week I returned, feeling embarrassed for unloading all my burdens on her the week before. She spoke softly, as she explained that she didn't think I was crazy or schizophrenic - her thought was that I was a natural born intuitive psychic.

This was the first time I had ever heard

these words. Of course, I had heard of psychics, but the thought never crossed my mind that I was one. In the coming weeks and months, she helped me to grow stronger. But I was still struggling to believe that I was a "natural born psychic." Until one session turned my world on its side.

My therapist asked me to tell her about her house and what it looked like. I was perplexed by this statement, and told her that I had no idea what her house looked like. She held her gaze on me and said "Yes you do. Tell me about my house." Scared to be put on the spot, I closed my eyes and just spoke about the images that were coming to me in my mind. "Your house is white." She replied with a yes. "It's two story and cape cod style"

She confirmed this as well.

"I see wildflowers and the tails of cats in the front porch—you must have several cats."

My therapist smiled at me and said, "Yes,

that is exactly right." She showed me pictures of her house at the end of the session. It was just as I had described. This experience helped me to believe in my abilities and overcome my last hurdle of denial.

I traded my diagnosis of crazy in for my new diagnosis of psychic.

With this new lease on life, I sought out all I could find to read about this psychic phenomenon. It felt like a homecoming, as I read about other people having experiences with the other side as I had. Never in my life had I suspected my vivid imagination to be an actual "talent" before now. It was just the only way I ever knew—a swirl of visions sounds and secrets. I thought I was simply a broken person not smart enough to focus and keep up with my peers. This was my real birth and beginning. I could now see how I had been lost in translation for so many years. Psychic had never been an option on the table before now. I knew that I was being touched by an angel with this new information, and it was my calling and destiny to find my way back to communicating with the other side.

Blessed After All/Growing Up in Two Worlds

Thirty years later, I am still seeing these lights and feeling the sounds. I have grown to understand this foreign language, and use it along with the images and insights I am shown to help other people gain perspective on their lives. I believe these lights and information to be from a higher realm. In all honesty, I wonder to myself everyday

"Why can I see them and feel them so clearly and others cannot? I'm just me…not Joan of Arc!"

It is difficult to hear this ability referred to as "Psychic" because I know this word can conjure images in people's minds of gypsies and crystal balls. For me, it is an organic way of life, and all that I have ever known. I use this ability currently, by weaving the psychic information that I am shown into the format of a counseling session. People come to me for life guidance and what I refer to as "Soul Interventions."

In these sessions, my goal is to help them locate and tune into their own inherent guidance system. Through this work, I relay to people a bigger picture and where they have strayed from the path. I often tell clients, "My job is to work myself out of a job." It's my privilege to bridge the gap between Guides and humans.

With Spirit Guides as my directors, I see events in the future and things that have happened to people in the past. I have found often that is not enough to make a true difference in people's lives unless they know how and where to apply the information given. In short, some mediums cross over the dead – I get to cross over the living!

Chapter 2

The Veil

What is The Veil?

The veil by its very nature is allusive, and represents the unknown. Sometimes it can be difficult to understand it's purpose or even harder yet to know when we have crossed into it. When you were a child, you may have heard someone describe the veil as the space between life and the afterlife-an etheric curtain that parts only for those who are transitioning out of the physical body. Of course, this sets the stage in our mind that none shall pass this boundary before we die; lending to our fear of premature access to what lies beyond.

It is not uncommon for children to have the natural capacity to see through the veil and experience sightings of spirits in the afterlife. As we age, this second sight seems to deteriorate in most of us. We recall the parting veil along with the inhabitants of the other side as just a hybrid of our fears blended with an overactive childhood imagination. Human beings are geared toward compartmentalization.

If information and ability is not applicable to our everyday life, or advancing us towards our future goals we automatically kick it to the back of our mind and store it deep in the vaults of our fading memory bank. As the old saying goes, "if you don't use it you lose it." It is only when we begin to question the unknown that the veil and its mystery re-nters our lives.

What lies beyond our world and how do we travel to this outlying territory? Are we safe to open the door to the other side? What happens if we go to the edge of reality? These questions and many more race through our minds when we consider the choice to push through what we have always known and believed- into a new world where impossibility becomes probability.

The veil to the other side is not a place or an exact location, but rather a threshold of belief. It resides in a state of consciousness that is accessed by tuning deeper into the subtle environment around you. This tuning process opens the door to an expanded reality that allows you to see, feel, hear and know beyond the barriers of the third dimension.

This ability to tune in to higher dimensions is the evolution of our thinking. It allows us to reach beyond our fixed reality and grow to know more about ourselves and the world around us. Gaining this insight is a vertical process, there are many layers to every single situation that you experience on a daily basis.

The deeper you go, the more you will experience life in a multidimensional state.

First Encounters

I was in 5th grade when I finally gained some understanding that what I was experiencing was a slipping back and forth between the veil. I often likened this experience to being like Superman. Just like Clark Kent who would enter the telephone booth a mortal man and emerge with new clothes and access to his super human abilities, I would toggle between seeing my teacher speaking to experiencing visions of myself standing in the middle of jungle warfare wearing war paint and motioning hand signals to my brothers in arms to follow close behind me. My teachers and parents did not see this ability like that of Superman's, but rather a daydreaming and focusing problem with a side of over indulged imagination.

One day the daydream became a reality. It was a normal morning in our class as we all rose, placed our hand over our heart, and began to recite the Pledge of Allegiance. Before I could get the first line "I pledge allegiance to the flag" out of my mouth, I began to see dirty camouflaged soldiers with heavy packs on their backs standing in our classroom. I was paralyzed as both of my worlds began to merge into one. The spirits of these men just hung there in a state of sadness while we spoke. As our class droned on reciting the anthem, the men slowly began to disappear from my sight leaving me with the overwhelming feeling of a heavy heart. I was almost able to keep my composure until the very end of the pledge when one of the boys in my classroom wadded up a piece of paper and threw it at me. That moment seemed to be the sum of all my totals; I burst into tears crying. My startled teacher called me to her desk and asked me what was wrong. I remember being shocked at the words that poured out of my heart and mouth.

I told her that we were not taking this anthem seriously, and it was important to really understand the sacrifices that were given for our country. I continued to cry uncontrollably as my heart broke for these forgotten men. My teacher walked me to the councilor's office where they called my mother. I was set out in my familiar hallway spot as the adults discussed yet another Bonni meltdown.

Hearing through the Veil

One day I decided to visit my little girl for lunch at her school. I admit that this is not exactly my favorite activity. I absolutely love children, but the elementary school I found to be intense and borderline uncomfortable with the amount of energy these little souls can pump out. Knowing this was what I was about to encounter, I decided to stop at the doors and pray for a deeper and more peaceful experience than what I was used to. When I approached the cafeteria, I was surprised to hear music pumping out of the room. To my knowledge, they never played music at lunch. In fact, the lunch staff was very focused on keeping the noise at a bare minimum.

This music took my breath away, it was like nothing I had ever heard before. It was a beautiful chaotic mix of symphony and heavy metallic melodies. I was beyond ecstatic that this little country town could be so progressive in their approach to child development. When I opened the lunchroom door, the music completely stopped. I was utterly confused as I walked to the nearest staff member and inquired about the music they had just been playing. I was told there had been no music playing, and that they never played music at lunchtime. The lunch lady must have thought I was crazy for asking such a thing. I stood and stared at the sea of animated chattering children for a moment when it finally hit me. They were the music I was hearing pouring out of the lunchroom walls. The frequency of the children's passionate conversation was a symphonic wonderland when tuned into on deeper level. This was a moment of expanded reality, and a perfect example of what's possible to experience beyond the topical layers of life. I wish that the poor lunch ladies could have multi-dimensional hearing like I had experienced, instead of the dreaded incessant loud voices they were in charge of muting.

Protection or Prison

Over the years I have spent working as a professional psychic medium I have had many clients tell me that they have been too scared to go to a psychic in the past in fear that they may hear something they didn't want to know or even worse, unlock the door to something evil.

This opens a very important topic. The veil has operated as protection for the masses since the beginning of time. This filtration process allows us to control our reality settings and manage our fears. I have been asked more times than I can count if I have ever encountered evil or demonic spirits. I answer their question with the following,

"The greatest universal rule is that of the law of attraction." The higher you keep your frequency the more positive your experience will be, and you will be more likely to attract high-vibrational beings rather than the heavier ones. It is the skinny jeans rule. If your energy is a size 2 skinny jeans vibration—no 900 -pound heavy spirit is going to want anything to do with trying to fit into your size 2 skinny jean frequency. They won't even shop at your store!

This doesn't mean that you should camp out in a haunted house, and all is guaranteed well if your high vibration equipped. It's just a good rule of thumb to lay your foundation on.

Simply Black and White

Over the years, I have worked with a few different paranormal investigation teams and have gone on many inquiries as their accompanying medium. I have seen things that even I had a hard time believing what was right before my eyes. I have been invited to investigate haunted homes, museums, caves, high schools, old buildings, camp sites, hospitals, old orphanages, asylums and even haunted pizza parlors. The one thing that each investigation has in common is that these are real stories of real people, and although they are no longer a part of the living they still care about the things they did while they were alive. Earthbound spirits are very rarely evil- most of them are just souls wanting to be heard so they can move on to the next phase of life in the afterlife. It is quite often that even after a spirit finds closure and crosses over, we can still feel the looming imprinted energy of pain they left behind. (This is extremely common on battlefields.) One of the most common mistakes is when people confuse residual pain as something that is potentially harmful or evil. Although imprinted pain energy can be very uncomfortable, it is not something that is looking to harm you. Your job is to stay above it!

In one instance, I was asked to join an investigation of an old mansion where a murder had supposedly occurred in the early 1900s. My good friend Samantha, who is a fellow medium, joined me on this case. Samantha is an amazing medium, beautiful inside and out. She is what most people expect a medium to look like, dressed in black gauzy lace with perfect thick black eyeliner against her porcelain skin. Samantha and I entered the house together and began walking the first floor. I immediately heard the sound of children's laughter and could smell the aroma of roasting turkey. I saw the face of a loving, rose cheeked old woman as she entered in to the kitchen. I turned around to check in with Samantha to see if she witnessed the old woman as well, when I noticed that she was bent over and propped up against a wall. When I asked her what was happening, it was all she could do to udder the words "Evil things are here."

I was incredibly perplexed. So far, I was picking up on the most heartwarming experiences from this old house. Samantha got her strength together and we climbed the stairs to the second floor. There was a different and darker energy radiating from the upstairs. One would almost experience this as sweltering humidity—that type of heaviness that just hangs in the air with nowhere to go. Samantha pointed to the corner of the largest room where she felt the strongest energy.

As we entered, it was clear to both of us that this was the room where the murder occurred. Although the energy was more stiff and stagnant than the rest of the house, we could see no trace of any lingering lost soul hanging around waiting to seek justice for his murder. There was just the painful imprinted energy of a situation where a life was taken too soon. Samantha and I made our way back down stairs with our notes in hand. She looked tired and limp like a wet dishtowel. She told me that she could feel the negative energy crawling over her body like hundreds of bugs and that she needed to leave immediately to go take a salt bath and pray. I felt terrible for her. When she asked how I was feeling all I could report was that I was incredibly hungry and felt a terrible craving for Applebee's.

This experience stands out to this day as a perfect example of the way we attract energy to ourselves and experience the other side. Although Samantha is a great medium, she had her sights set on looking for the worst-case scenario, and ultimately found it within just a few minutes. The moral of this story is that we both came out accessing the same information, but only one of us had to suffer to retrieve it. If you go looking for the ugly side of the other side you will usually find what you are looking for.

The Thinning

We are moving into the intuitive age as a byproduct of our human evolution. Communication has become faster and faster and we are experiencing the shortening of the English language. Our children are speaking fragments of words and full sentences are already a thing of the past. If you cannot communicate your point in five words or less to your children, you will be left behind. Some may see this as a degeneration and laziness on the part of our all-star next generation of adults, and in some cases, this may be true. But what is happening on a larger scale is that human beings are speeding up to prepare for the thinning of the veil.

It has been said that no teacher will come before the student is ready. A perfect example of a teacher coming to the mass students is Jesus. Some scientists believe that there was a seven percent spike in our evolution during the time of Christ's teachings. People were ready and in great need of his love and direction. The thinning of the veil means that we are in fact ready for the next phase of learning and inter-dimensional life experiences. The filters are slowly lifting as we expand and hold on to more information, and communicate in a deeper way with those benevolent sources who have been guiding us gently from behind closed doors.

Our individual and collective teachers are stepping forward to shine a light on the purpose of our soul's contract and help us with the ability to communicate with your highest self.

Many of our children are coming in with an updated understanding of this telepathic communication. They are highly empathic and can give and receive volumes of information within a matter of seconds. Some children have delayed speech and interaction with other people for this very reason. As the intuitive age unfolds, this sixth sense becomes less of an oddity and more of a necessity to understand the psychic exchange we have with each other and the environment around us—if not for ourselves, then for the survival of our children in an increasingly difficult and divided planet.

More and more people who have never considered themselves to be psychic have been reaching out to me to help them understand these almost overnight changes they are experiencing in their life. They are beginning to see spirits in the afterlife, feel a roller coaster of emotions and sensations that they can't explain, as well as an increasingly active night life where their dreams are becoming more vivid and bizarre. I have been asked if this the "second coming." I tell them that I know this thinning of the veil is the next stage of our evolution and it is coming. So, if that's the second coming then, yes!

As the veil thins, we will be able to see, feel and hear more of the happenings of other dimensions. This does not have to be a frightening experience if you remember these three things.

1- God will never give us more than we can handle.

2- Just because it's a dark shadow does not mean that it is automatically evil. (Energy comes in many forms—don't discriminate.)

3- You are an inter-dimensional human with divine protection and you are preparing to see who you really are and where you came from.

The Human Pinball Machine

As we increase our intuitive abilities and more of the unknown penetrates our daily lives, it helps to know how the information comes into your awareness. We are exposed to incoming information through our senses—what we know, what we feel, what we hear, and what we see. We are a walking talking body full of all our experiences and hard lessons that we have encountered throughout our lifetime. Often, we can be quick to make judgments about the unknown due to the defensive protection that we have put up to survive the pain we have encountered. Even the nicest, most happy-go-lucky person has been forever altered to some degree by their pain. This is the nature of our human experience. When information from your guides and higher self comes to you, it can be met with resistance due to its seemingly foreign nature. It hits the senses that communicate with your nervous system. This is a highly subconscious process. As information comes to you, it is much like a game of human pinball—the transmitted message from your guide bounces off your life experience, hits your trust meter and shoots past your internal bodyguard for your pain. Once the information ball reaches the bottom, the message can sometimes be tainted or changed almost entirely.

This is very similar to that telephone game we played in school as children where one child whispered a message into the ear of the next child and the information was passed from child to child until the end where it was almost always revealed as completely different than the original message. Sometimes you can start with a lamb and end up with the message of a blood hungry lion. It happens.

The good news is that there are techniques and skills that you can apply to help you retain the original content of your message. It is important for us to better understand our original nature and predisposition, to better serve us in this uncharted growth process of surviving and thriving in the intuitive age.

The Reality Shift
Part 1 of the shift: CHASING NORMAL

No matter what we try to tell ourselves about what is logical and sane, we all have those moments when we question our sanity. We will contemplate the ratio of imagination to reality and bat around the idea of just how far we are willing to go down the rabbit hole of the sixth sense. Many of us have been taught that psychic phenomenon is a slippery slope, and if you open that door, there is more than likely a chance that you would not be able to close it.

You may find that you have spent a lifetime trying to develop and harness your intuitive nature and have been met with a handful of interesting and unexplainable experiences, while still left feeling at a loss on how it connects to the larger purpose of your life. Intuitive development is like someone giving you the keys to a brand-new Ferrari. You realize you have the ability take off and reach a hundred miles per hour in sixty seconds, only to find yourself shortly thereafter stuck in standstill rush hour traffic. The ability to achieve a successful intuitive lifestyle is found in a very personal yet profound place: your expectations of normal.

We don't like to mess with our speed settings. Our days find their way into a routine and our jobs and relationships begin to fall into patterns and ruts like clockwork. We like to stay within the boundaries of what we know and understand because this allow us to feel safe and secure. This plan works until a wave of change strikes and we find ourselves scrambling to put the pieces back together in hopes to once again meet our standard of normal. We like normal. Change scares us. The problem with normal is that it becomes our identity which is stuck in a cycle of last season's reruns. Our daily patterns are set to the standards of our expectations. We are masters of filling up space and time, and leaving little to no room for the magic of the unexpected. If we open and allow our normal to break free, to the possibility of the limitless world of intuition, we may feel that the sense of security is the first to escape through the cracks. We are faced with momentous urge to turn back to what we have known and what has worked for us in the past.

Ultimately, our need for normal and predictable can outweigh our want for the journey of the unshackled intuitive driven life. Other reasons we choose to stay in our box is to avoid the unleashing of our personal pain. Pain is a shape shifter, although it is coming from the same root it changes its identity and presents itself differently every day .Traces of our painful past can be found in just about every aspect of our lives. We can be in the best possible mood and all it takes is one reckless and rude driver on the road to send us spiraling into a series of scared, angry and judgmental thoughts. Sometimes our pain emerges without any prompt or warning. Have you ever been going about your day, and suddenly had a flashback of a memory from your past when you were denied something you wanted, or a memory when someone in your life who has hurt you and the anger and sadness reconnects with your brain almost as strongly as it did when the actual event took place? Our heart and brain stores memories of pain. We don't always know the correct channels of forgiving or releasing this pain so we bottle it up, close the door and bury the key deep in our internal cellars. Our "Normal" is the watcher and keeper of this pain. Normal insures that nothing much wiggles to the surface escaping its cold, dark room. The cost of such a disruption may create additional pain and bring chaos to our relationships, jobs, or worse –a falling out with our perception of ourselves. Our normal believes the best case scenario is that only our manageable pain escapes the cellar.

It is much easier in the moment to suppress and downgrade the emotional storms to daily annoyances, small rants and mist eyes instead of full blown meltdowns and long crying spells.

Releasing the Old Normal

The stories we continue to tell ourselves are largely built on the foundation of our past. Those times in life when we experienced loss or pain from personal trauma and tragedy have remained with us on a deep cellular level. We are living libraries that are in no way limited to just our painful experiences, but a collection of all life's encounters. Our foundation is also a keeper of our beautiful, sacred, soul-strengthening memories that keep us connected to a greater experience of divine wholeness. These happy moments can act as a springboard back to a lighter version of ourselves if we call upon them to re-enter our mind. Although most anyone would agree that they would rather live from a root of happy memories instead of the painful ones, the reality is that each one of us is driven by the loudest voice behind our feelings and emotions. Pain that has yet to be released will continue with its dominance inside of our mind, body and spirit. This pain needs to be released in order to enter into your highest intuitive state.

So, where do we go from here? We begin by pulling the weeds out of our beautiful mind garden. If you have ever planted a garden or a flowerbed, then you know that your perfect outdoor creation only lasts a few weeks before unwanted intruders breach the barriers of beauty. Weeds begin to multiply almost by the minute, choking out the life of your garden. We could cover the weeds with dirt or cut the stocks with scissors, but this would be a short-term topical fix to a larger problem. Although our garden would return to its original external beautiful state, just below the surface a war is being waged: a battle for life and death. The only way to truly restore the health of these plants would be to kill the weeds off completely. There are two ways to remove weeds and stop them from taking over your garden.

The first is to spray them with chemicals. This is effective and gets the job done in a short time with minimal effort. However, you are adding chemicals to the soil your plants are using for a source of nutrients and this may alter the vitality of your garden.

The second removal method is to pull the weeds out of the ground all the way to the root. This can take an abundance of time and energy but allows your garden to continue to grow and thrive in its natural progression of life stages.

Your mind is no different than your garden. We want the seeds of our mind to thrive in its growth cycles and become something extraordinary and beautiful. We are tempted to cover up our pain weeds with topical fixes or in some instances, we take the route of chemical extermination. Just as in the garden, our mind will benefit greatly from connecting to the root of our pain and working to pull it out. This process may take time and energy, but it is a price that will repay itself again and again over your present and future days. We will talk more about how to release your pain and pull the weeds later in this book.

Chapter 3

You Are Not Alone: Contact with Guides and Guardians

A Forever Love

In the beginning, before you make the journey into life you have a plan. A contract with God, with the purpose of advancing your soul's knowledge through the experiences you will encounter in your lifetime. Pain and pleasure both have its perfect place in this tapestry of our existence. Your plan has multiple options but they will all lead you to your ultimate destination.

Sounds simple enough, right?

It would be simple if we could consciously remember the contract and itinerary always ensuring that we stay focused and on the right path. We are born with our beautiful memories of the other side wiped from our slate. Who in their right mind came up with this rule you may ask. It seems cruel and unnecessary to leave us stranded in the dark when so much is at stake.

This in fact was not a terrible trick placed upon humans, but a chance of a lifetime. Many souls never even incarnate into life on Earth, so if you are here, consider yourself an elite soul with the courage to take on what many don't yet have the strength for. Just by being born, you are half way to the finish line! Now that's a great head start!

It is our job here on Earth to wake up to the bigger plan of our soul's contract. We need to keep faith as a touchstone, hold our head up through all the twists and turns, and believe in something larger than ourselves allowing us to surrender to the flow of life that is the divine director of our spiritual goals.

This journey we are partaking in is not a journey of one. We all have our own pit crew and they are referred to as your "Guides" and "Guardians." This life of yours is divinely guided by benevolent beings that love you unconditionally. There is nothing you have ever done, or will ever do to turn them away from you and break this loving sacred bond. You are never unattended. Someone has always been at your side. Even at your darkest hour when you felt all alone, you had a silent partner.

I have heard more times than I can count people telling me that their guides must be out for an "extended lunch break," or "on vacation in the Bahamas." They can't feel any assistance and feel forgotten and lost. Also, if they had guides and guardians that were present, why would these all-knowing beings have allowed such a wrong turn to occur.

This outlook is completely understandable and often when we need guidance the most, that's when we can block our own heavenly guided feedback. The hard truth about these guides is that they will not stand in the way of our free will. They are subtle directors that are here to lead your life with you—not for you. They speak a soft language that can be heard internally and externally if you just know how to listen to this ethereal communication.

A Thousand Years

One of the first workshops I ever lead was on how guides communicate with us in our everyday lives. I was absolutely "Nervecited!" (the amazing combination of being simultaneously nervous and excited). To better prepare myself for the class I had the idea to make a list to try to anticipate all the questions people may have about the world of Spirit Guides. My list was coming together quite nicely with a range of questions from "Are my guides with me in the bathroom?" to

"Can my guide be my deceased Grandmother?" When I came to the final question, I wanted to add to my list "How long have we known our Guides and been assigned to them?"

The strangest thing happened to me at that moment.... absolutely nothing! I didn't have any internalized answer to that question. It was like having "mind crickets" nothing came in response. My whole life I have had quite a knack for asking questions, but not necessarily the equivalent ability of patience to wait and hear the answers. I decided to be patient to the best of my ability; still nothing came. I wondered if this question was unanswerable. Even louder than the silence I had a feeling I was being set up for a teachable moment in "Guideology."

I waited for several minutes for my answer, and right before I was ready to throw in the towel on my question, I had a thought enter my mind. I should go turn on the radio, and that will be my answer. Grateful for some guidance, I jumped up and switched on the radio. The song that came pumping through the speakers was a Christina Perry song from the movie "Twilight." The words that immediately hit my ears were "I loved you for a thousand years I will love you for a thousand more." The song brought me to tears and sent shivers through my whole body.

Accident? I think not! Small moments such as these add up to a big relationship with your Guides.

Our simple thoughts are quite often dictation from our spiritual advisors. They come as thoughts in our head in the tone of our own voice. When we learn to hear the quiet words behind our loud thoughts, it is then when we tap into the messages from our Guides and Guardians.

The morning of the workshop, I had "thoughts" about needing to include white feathers in the class. I had no idea how or why

I needed to incorporate white feathers, but I figured I had better heed this divine direction. I stopped at store after store looking for white feathers and continued to come up empty handed.

It is in those times when you're trying to follow guidance and it continues to not work out that you really begin to doubt your sanity! As time ran down to the wire, I had one last idea on where to find white feathers. The thought that was coming to me was to return to the first store I stopped at earlier in the morning. Feeling crazy, I continued to follow the breadcrumbs back to where I began, only to find that they had just restocked the white feathers on a shelf that was empty a few hours before! I bought all of them still feeling uncomfortable with the fact that I had no idea what they were for.

When I reached the building where I would be teaching the workshop, the last piece of the puzzle floated quietly into my mind. I should place feathers on the ground leading from the front door all the way up the staircase and on each one of the chairs to introduce the greatest love story of all time. The love between worlds was received as people entered the room clutching the white feathers they found on their way up. There was no question in my mind that this workshop was divinely lead. Once the class was over, three separate people took me aside and confided that they had just prayed for a sign that morning to know that they were being watched over, and specifically asked to find a confirmation in the form of a white feather.

I learned that day that the moment when you think love has found the brim, your cup can still run over.

Earth School

Remember that old comedy standup routine "Who's on first"? That is exactly what it feels like when we try and make "logical" sense of the placement of guides and people within our life. We are taught that we are supposed to love thy neighbor and be a good person, but even when we try to do everything right sometimes our neighbor still hates us and tries to make our life miserable. Equally frustrating, is when we are trying to be our most empathetic, compassionate self and our guides seem to check out, allowing aggressive and mean people to break through the gate of our peaceful and well intentioned bubble.

Where is the reward and purpose in all of this? It all comes down to that very important initial agenda of dedicating your life to the making of an evolved superhuman!

You made your Guides promise no matter how loud you screamed "uncle" during times of extreme trial they would support you in achieving the "higher" goals you set for yourself in this lifetime. This is all about the final product of your soul's evolution. Through well placed learning platforms we grow and stretch into this expanded soul we set out to become. During times of pain and chaos, it is more important than ever to remember that there are no accidents and all things are a vital part of your soul's plan. Even the unbelievably rude, inconsiderate, selfish, practically intolerable family members, friends, neighbors and all of life's meltdown moments are shaping you for the better if you stay focused and willing to see the diamond in the rough.

Earth is very much like a school that we are all attending with a variety of different grades. You may be in high school learning advanced spiritual lessons and dating someone in elementary school who is still working on getting down the basics. This presents a large problem on the surface, but higher up the chain this is the perfect soul solution for both of you. When we finally understand the lessons, it is then we will be prepared to move on to the next evolutionary platform. The teacher will always come when the student is ready—and sometimes the teacher is in a lower grade than you are. If it sounds like a whole lot of work, it is, but it is well worth it!

Higher Dimensions

The idea of school and higher levels of understanding is also present on the other side. Each dimension embraces its different teachers and collective information. If we wanted to go straight to the source which many of us understand to be God, we could but would be met with the limitations of being human and most of the information would be inconceivable to our limited minds. From God we receive love and seek other intelligences to interpret the rest of the plan.

Angels are not far from God. They are easier to receive information from, but it is not always somewhere we can find answers to our more specific questions. For example, if you ask the angels "Why did I lose my job and how am I going to make my house payment this month?" They often respond with some variation of "All is well my child. You are loved by God. Have faith." That is of course completely true! However, that doesn't explain how we are going to manage paying the mortgage. Angels are always right in the end, but there can just be an unnerving lack of details in the meantime!

Below the Angels, there are many other dimensions where guides and teachers reside. These benevolent messengers are closer to the human race by design. Spiritual Guides can communicate with details and give more specific direction. Understanding the human plight is their specialty. As bilingual beings, they have the ability to carry the will of God, and your higher selves' agenda while managing your amnesia stricken third dimensional human self. They truly are the celestial acrobatics!

As you evolve through your individual life lessons, you will often obtain new Guides scheduled for your next phase of learning. It is very common for people to experience personality and preference shifts when new guides come in. When in alignment with their energy, we will take on the characteristics of our spirit guides. If you can recall a time when you became obsessed with a seemingly random hobby, new area of study or even radical change in clothing style, that was most likely a time when you underwent a guide shift.

Destiny for a Moment

Several years ago, I was sitting on the couch watching TV when an overwhelming sensation came over me. I felt with every fiber of my being that I was meant to be a yoga teacher—it was my destiny! I had only done yoga 3 times in my entire life. So naturally, this seemed like an odd conviction to those around me. That night I signed up with no hesitation to a yoga training facility that I had never visited, with teachers who taught yoga styles I could barely pronounce. Although the training was pricey, I considered it a value that I would never regret.

The first day it was quite evident that I was in way over my head. The people in this class had been studying yoga for a decade or more working up to this teacher training.

After the first class, I went for a walk and cried my heart out to a nearby oak tree so I wouldn't take this devastation back to my family. Desperately, I asked the tree if it had any advice and the only thought I had come back was to "stay the course no matter how out of place I felt." Feeling ridiculous about heeding the advice of a tree I decided that really the only thing I could do was to stay and just see where it took me. Slowly but surely, I began to catch up and hang on for dear life.

One day when it came time to learn yoga philosophy in the class, everything shifted and I immediately felt a homecoming. As we read the sacred yogic texts, I felt like a pregnant woman craving ice cream, sardines and pickles—it didn't really make sense, I just knew I wanted more of it! My Amazon account became overloaded with queued books on Buddhism and biographies of yogic gurus.

After the training, I opened my own local yoga practice and as some destinies do, it came and went within 6 months' time. Although short lived, I still consider this to be one of the most pivotal times in my life. A few months after I closed the practice I met a medium friend of mine for lunch. She laughed when I approached her outside the restaurant. When I asked her what was so funny, she replied "Well someone got a new swami guide since I've seen them last... I bet you have been obsessed with yoga!" My short-lived destiny all clicked together with that statement. I learned at that moment just how much you can merge with your Guides' energy!

What is the other side?

The other side is a continuation of many dimensions beyond ours that are teaming with life and living in an expanded reality experience. We are in the 3rd dimension, as we go up the evolution education system, we have the 4th dimensions, 5th dimensions, the 6th dimensions, and so forth. It is commonly believed that heaven as we know it, is the next closest dimension found in the 4th dimension. This can explain why our earliest experiences of seeing through the veil have been contact with deceased loved ones, as well as sightings of anonymous spirits floating by unaware of our existence.

Our 3D reality is connected to time. The other side and upper dimensions beyond the veil are connected to space.

If we are not yet ready to expand into our deepest spiritual path, the veil holds firm and we fill up our days with unending tasks to keep us in the box of our 3D life. It is a type of protection and a stage of denial that keeps us on the ground and focused only on only what we think is relevant to our daily lives. When we slow down and tune in to a deep place of the soul's core purpose, we disconnect from time and cross over into space.

The souls purpose can be better understood if we begin by becoming familiar with our chosen archetype.

Wisdom Keepers and Warriors (Archetypes)

An Archetype is like a file folder that holds all the specific talents and lessons that your soul chooses to experience under one large umbrella. They are the magnetic life themes that draw people, places, and situations into our lives so that we can get down to business and meet our full potential. Often, people will have a joint archetype to accelerate their opportunities to grow as spiritual beings in a bodily experience. Archetypes are not far from how we experienced high school where everyone sectioned off into the jocks, artists, cheerleaders, theater nerds, brainiacs, and of course the "herbalist" crowd.

Warriors

Strange but true, the perfect match for me happens to be my husband of fifteen years who has a career in law enforcement and holds the position of a sniper on a swat team. He has had many positions over the years within the police department and has the strongest honor bound integrity of anyone I have ever met. He is a gentle giant with an old soul and a warrior's heart that would defend your life or rescue a turtle in the middle of the road at any given moment.

I will never forget the day that my husband told me about the creed that the military and law enforcement men and women follow. He said "There are three types of people in the world: sheepdogs, sheep, and wolves. The sheepdogs are the warriors that are born to protect and serve. The sheep are the people in the world living many different callings but who do not feel called to be a warrior and then there are the wolves. The wolves are the people that are out for themselves and look to prey on the sheep." Sheepdogs will dedicate their lives to protect the innocent sheep and keep them safe from the hungry wolves.

If you are a warrior archetype, you probably already know it. You're the brave heart that will stand up for the underdog and seek justice. You are paired with guides that represent a similar purpose. It is not uncommon for me to meet someone with a warrior's archetype and see a band of Native American Indian Guides around them. You are honor bound and born to preserve the innocent and goodness of our planet.

Healers

Healer archetypes are born with the natural gift to heal others. They are usually highly sensitive and empathic souls who can't help but open their hearts to the sick and misfortunate people of the world. Healers can channel healing energy from Guides, Angels, and God organically and are often unaware they are affecting such radical change and healing on the people around them. They are balls of light that roam the planet within many different careers and stations such as hairdressers, social workers, nurses, doctors, teachers, waiters, parents, artists, ministers, to name only a few. The oath of a healer is to "heal and do no harm" people under this archetype often suffer from guilt, always worried they have not done enough to help or spoke and acted in a "wrong" way. The healers are the humanitarian Mother Teresa's of our world and are guided by high vibrational beings to help build the bridge between Heaven and Earth.

Engineers

Engineer archetypes are our builders and fixers. Their minds are always going a mile a minute. Fixing problems and finding solutions, that is what makes their world go around. They usually are highly creative and innovative people who are always five steps ahead of everyone around them. This archetype was responsible for our early freemasons and ancient builders, those who were channeling change before the world even knew what it needed or what it could become. At their best, these people are focused on syncing their minds and hearts and following the combined content to the final outcome. My experience of people with Engineer archetypes is that they are highly intelligent people that can be often misunderstood due to their ability to have one foot in this world and the other foot in another reality or dimension. If you happened be dating or married to an Engineer archetype, it is my best advice to you to pray for patience as you can sometimes be the last person visited on this mental paper route they are divinely running.

Artist

The Artist archetypes are the worlds intuitive visionaries. They are the seers and seekers of beauty. Artist people can repurpose almost anything and restore hope in others with their ability to shape emotion into matter. They can be the vehicle for expressing what is beyond the boundaries of our third dimension with use of tools such as words, colors, sound, and texture. We have all had that experience of awe connecting to a certain song, painting, sculpture, food, building, and even down to our clothes. That awe is the talent this archetype exposes for us so that we can become inspired to reconnect to our own individual core gifts and abilities. These people are simply born to rouse the visionary in all, and introduce new ways of seeing magic in the mundane.

Wisdom Keepers

Think back for a moment to the teacher, neighbor, nanny or loved one that had the greatest impact on your life. That was most likely someone who held the Wisdom Keeper archetype. These people impact lives in big ways. They are the philosophers, storytellers, leaders, and missionaries that can see who you are at your core. Wisdom Keepers often have Ascended Masters as Spiritual Guides, and can direct you back to your own soul contracts. These people can summarize the planet and emote an energetic blueprint for united living. Wisdom Keepers are the oldest of souls and often can be found teaching about faith, love and miracles. If you are missing a parental figure in your life, or feel that you have lost your direction, ask your Guides to send a Wisdom Keeper on your path to bring you back to the space where your true self resides.

We are the Human Time Capsules - Higher self and Past Lives

Our higher self is all things that we can't retain and remember about our soul's plan, but continue experiencing anyway on a regular basis. It is everything and everywhere we are. It is our multidimensional self-living in an expanded reality.

Our higher self is found in a deeper state of perceiving. Finding this space requires our attention to our soul's core that is found in the details and patterns inside and outside of us that are present in our everyday life. In a nutshell, the other side is just where your highest potential self hangs out until you realize it exists. Think for a moment about the person you were five or even ten years ago. Did that person have any clue how the person you are now would be? How many times have you said, "If you would have told me five years ago I would be doing this, I would have thought you were crazy!" Where was the part of your soul that was waiting for you to fulfill that seemingly crazy plan? All the versions of you already exist. They're just there waiting for you to grow into them.

Human Time Capsules

We are human time capsules and a storehouse for more information than we ever would have imagined. Scientists are now finding that we hold the life experiences of our ancestors inside our DNA as a part of our personal genetic memory. It makes you wonder if grandma believing she couldn't lose her extra biscuits and gravy weight is the reason you hang onto those extra ten pounds! We have considered the physical DNA markers; now it is time to introduce the idea of "mental markers."

Our soul has lived many physically incarnated lifetimes taking us to new lands and limits so that we can experience life in countless different arenas. When I ask people if they believe in the possibility of past lives it is very rare that I hear a fixed "no." Most people are at least open to the idea of past lives and report that they haven't ever really put much thought into it. If past lives are real and I believe that they are, It really wouldn't do us any good if we couldn't retain at least some of the information about our experiences. Our lives are like chapters in a book. Each chapter has a new and different theme connecting to the last chapter and setting up for the one to come.

As a hypnotherapist, I have performed countless past life regressions and the one thing they all seem to have in common is the strong emotions that emerge during the regression. People are shocked that they could emotionally bond and react to the images playing out in their head that have seemingly little to no reference to their current life. I have often been told by clients that experiences encountered during a past life regression seemed so close yet so far away. They always knew these were the challenges that were holding them back in their current life, but could come to no logical reason why.

Our afflictions from our past lives, especially when gone unresolved can carry through to our current life embedded deep within our cellular memory.

A New Child

One of my projects for the training program to become a certified hypnotherapist was to regress someone who had never had a regression experience before. My brave little 11 year old daughter was my first pick. Although my daughter was a tomboy and a tough kid, she suffered from some significant anxieties. She had always been fearful that one day I was going to leave her and never return. My daughter grew increasingly more shy around adults and was often clinging to my side. The other strange fear she had was related to sports. She loved sports; especially soccer. My daughter begged to try softball as well. After we joined the team she developed a strong aversion to holding the bat. She would become highly nervous. We figured it was a form of performance anxiety although she had not shown these signs in any of her other activities.

I did not have any set expectations for my daughter's regression. Honestly, at the time I didn't even think about doing a regression on her to help with the anxieties. I was just trying to complete the project and pass the class.

With little explanation on what to expect I began the past life regression on my daughter. She struggled to see anything in the beginning and then all at once it was like you opened the flood gates on a made for TV movie. My daughter began to explain in detail about the rundown house she was living in with her younger brother and father in poverty. She told me that she was a 14-year-old boy and life was hard because their mother just left one day years earlier and had not been seen since. My daughter felt that her father struggled to make ends meet and stayed in a stressed out and quick to temper state. As we moved forward, she continued with accounting more of the same-struggle and tension in this family until we came to the last day of her life.

She saw herself as a 16-year-old boy walking, wearing an "orange backpack". One evening on the way home she saw him cutting through a baseball field, where he encountered a gang. Before I could bring her out of the regression she witnessed herself being beat to death with baseball bats. I was horrified that I had just put my child through the viewing of such a vicious attack. I guess I was hoping she would regress back to a lifetime where she passes gently in her sleep at 99. To my astonishment my daughter came out of the regression excited as if we had just stumbled upon a cure for everything from cavities to cancer. She talked rapidly about the emotions she had experienced in this altered state. It was almost like her soul knew that this was what it had been seeking and awaiting closure for. That day was the last day of her riddling anxiety.

It was like I had a new child!

My now 19-year-old daughter will still testify to that regression being one of the most significant and healing days of her life. (although she still detests orange backpacks)

Just the shear act of visiting that lifetime allowed the boogie man to step out of the closet and into the light- never to haunt her again.

This and many other past life regressions are what helped me to finally understand exactly what people mean when they say, "knowledge is power."

Soul Records

As you can see we resubmit ourselves life after life to achieve the most precious virtues and restore balance to our own polarities. All our chapters are stored in a collection of records known as the "Akasha." It is our birthright to be able to tap into the Akashic records whenever we choose. This personal journey doesn't only affect our own life, but generations to come. With each experience, we touch a piece of this world that will forever be recognized and recorded. The gravity of this gift may only fully be known when we are willing to remember what we have forgotten and reach out for the heavenly guidance of our spirit guides. They are closest to our soul records and can help us quickly recover if we have gotten lost on our path. We will never attend our Earth classes alone.

Chapter 4

Inside and Out: The Purpose of Your Soul's Journey to Earth

The Contract

Imagine for a moment you and a council of your Guides sitting around a large conference table with a long map rolled out on the table before you. This map is old and marked with a timeline of the years you would embark on your journey into life. You hear your Guides speak about the talents you will embody, as well as the trials you will face. It is explained to you that you are in the running of the bravest souls and this paper represents your commitment to… Oh, rats! You can't remember can you? That's the point! Through faith and reconnection to your core you will recall the purpose of your driven soul. The key to remembering the magic of this road map is found in the simplest corners of your beginnings.

Remember when you were little and you would do just about anything to please your parents? I remember lying in bed as a little girl trying to come up with ways to make my mother proud of me. My list included extra chores, being outwardly polite to strangers, better school grades and of course keeping my problematic "over imagination" to myself. As a child, I seemed quite convinced that everything you do is for the benefit of pleasing parents. My mother told me that when I was around 4 years old I would gaze up at the beautiful pink sunsets in Nevada and say "Look at that sky! God's mom is going to be so proud of him!"

As I grew older, I became less interested in pleasing my parents and became more focused on pleasing God. Even in my preteen to teenage years I felt the contract that was inside of me. The will to live to my greatest God potential got me out of bed most days. This of course occurred on my better days. There were also days when I wondered if I was even connected at all and if I belonged on the planet. I began this life being raised in a loosely Jewish household and from there discovered and committed to several different Christian churches and even to the Mormon faith for a brief period. I thrived in church no matter what religion I was at the moment. This gave me hope along with a straightforward rulebook on how to be a good person, as well as scratching the itch I had for God pleasing.

Religion was truly the prerequisite for finding my goodness. This worked for many years until I was a young adult with children. I began having odd experiences when praying, such as flashes of light and color—

similarly to what I would see as a child when I would go to bed at night. The fear was setting in once again that I would not fit into the crowd; not even the church crowd. I began researching religion and the Bible to its core, looking for something that would include my abnormalities. Within my search, I uncovered many theological truths that had been omitted from the Bible. Past lives being one of them that was removed.

I was heartbroken. I took my pain to my preacher. This woman was one of the strongest most God driven people I have ever known. I collapsed my bleeding heart on her doorstep with every feeling from not fitting in, to my sadness of the altered bible. My preacher told me that evening I had "The faith of a 5 year old and that it was a gift not everyone had." At this point, I wasn't sure if she was complimenting or condemning me. She went on to explain that the love and commitment I felt was the gift I had to offer and that many people use church as a ritual, not as a rite of passage. In so many words, my preacher inferred that I may have outgrown the church and should dig deeper to better understand my soul contract and purpose.

How do we tap into our contract? We have had so many life experiences that have sent us in dozens of directions. Where do we begin unraveling the tangles of life? It may sound too simple to be true, but we tap into our contract by going back to the beginning. What did you want to be when you grew up? Who were your favorite people and friends? What broke your heart when you didn't get what you wanted or needed? What were your favorite toys and games? Where did you find the most peace?

As you dig deeper back into your early years when you were fresh off Heaven's press- take a look inside of your beginning. The child you were will help you unfold the story and make sense of your purpose. Our tendency is to want to run outside of ourselves and escape while pushing blame on irresponsible family members and unfortunate life events. When you go back to the beginning, you can retrieve the core of who you are by staying focused on what was happening on the inside of your child more than the outside. These answers will give you a strong foundation to build on, and a gateway to access your original blueprint. Just remember to keep it simple and go back to the beginning!

Keeping the Rhythm and Flow

Have you ever experienced life in a state of flow, where all the pieces fall into just the right places at the perfect moment? If you have known how good life can be when it is in the utopian state of flow, then you most likely understand why you try so hard to keep it there, or get it back if it falls out of this divine synchronization. You can't butter up the big guy and make this flow thing happen, nor can you drift through life and just let the pieces fall. Flow is born from the perfect balance of heeding your calling while surrendering to any uncertainty about the outcome.

Fear is the number one killer of flow. Our guides will send us repeated messages in the form of thoughts and synchronicity imploring us to make a move and fear can interrupt the directives that are being sent our way. If you are unhappy, most likely something is out of balance and out of flow and to add insult to injury, the imbalance may not even be within the very thing or situation you are unhappy about.

To stay in the flow of life you need to become familiar with the idea of cycles. Everything in your life has a pattern and purpose. Although you may feel sometimes like a scattered hot mess, your line of travel is straight as an arrow from the perspective of the other side. Cycles will run through your life in this order: 1 birth, 2 growth, 3 wrap–up, 4 death.

If you are present and operating within the correct phase of the cycle, then you will have a centering and experience a state of flow. Problem and loss of rhythm arise when we become fearful to leave a stage in the cycle behind. For example, let's say you opened a successful used bookstore and you stayed in the flow from first conception of the idea through the growth of a now thriving business. You have created an intimate setting that draws the locals in to curl up with a good book. People and books keep coming and your tiny store is starting to feel claustrophobic, not to mention your job is getting more difficult as you try to keep maximizing your space. You recently have been getting signs and messages to move down the road to a larger space.

You are officially in the natural wrap up phase of this cycle, however you are too scared to make any changes because people love and adore the space you created, and business is still good. What if you lose everything if you change the formula?

Life and its cycles move forward with or without you. There is a death coming to this small space to make room for the next birth of a larger one. If you were to hang on to this business as it was and refused to move with the cycles, death could come in another way. Your shop would begin to feel uncomfortable and out of flow to your customers and the business would take a nosedive, ultimately resulting in you closing your doors and leaving the building behind just the same -but with harder knocks.

We are evolving beings in the constant cycle of evolution. We are designed to move with the flow and have faith that death doesn't always mean the end of all life, just an end of a cycle. The tricky thing with cycles and flow is timing. Sometimes a life cycle spans over a decade and others over the course of a few months. It is important to stay present and focused and master the art of cycle surfing to maintain the flow of life!

Begin by looking where unhappiness has crept into your life and trace it back to the stage of the cycle it is currently in. Get to the bottom of the fear or lethargy that is dragging on any phase that should be released. Keep the faith that your life can find the flow once again. Our life doesn't need to be a state of rhythm and blues!

Faith Formula: It is All About Believing

Religion was my nest, and belief in my intuition became my wings to fly beyond the nest. As the veil continues to thin, we will encounter phenomenon like we have never experienced before. Our senses are being raised and cultivated to experience life in a 5-dimensional world far beyond the 3-dimensional world we currently live within. This means that we are at a point in our evolution where we need to be willing to fly beyond the nest and meet our evolving realities. This can be a scary process if you are not sure where the safety net lies. Faith is your net, and your willingness to believe is your acceleration to fly. If you can't believe what you will be seeing or experiencing and have faith in the net that will catch you if you fall, it will be difficult to ever leave the nest.

Believe It to See It

The first thing I tell my clients when I am training them to open their intuitive abilities it that imagination is real. Intuition and imagination are interchangeable. All energy comes from somewhere not from nowhere. It is the receiving side of your brain that can capture things outside what is deemed possible. Your guides work through "imagination" to drop information into the portals of your mind. You can become trapped in a loop if you are stuck in thinking you are just making up what you are seeing, and never move past your own threshold. When you were young, someone most likely inferred or just flat out told you that your imagination was not real. This is how we learn early on to separate the possible from the impossible.

Our analytical left brain is like a bouncer at a nightclub. It is responsible for only letting in information that will help you fit in and be a part of your social surroundings. It's got your back when it comes to weeding out anything that will make you look too weird. The difficulty that arises from our nightclub bouncer is that once it is told that imagination is not real. It records the sensation that is fired off every time you would believe beyond or use your imagination and alerts the mind that "this is not real." This process would occur hundreds and hundreds of times causing you to reroute neural pathways, and calcify the gateways to your imagination and natural receiver to the other side.

The formula to move forward and break down these walls to your intuition is to stand firm on what you know before you leap. Take a personal faith accounting and get to the bottom of what you truly believe in your heart. Do you believe that God is the director of your pursuits? Are you safe to explore past the boundaries of the world you have always known? Do you believe there is more than what you have been told? Do you have faith that you will return from your journey and be comfortable with the information you have gained?

Catch and Release: The Brain Bypass

Once you feel safe, you can then begin opening the door to the beyond. Trust is the cornerstone of your intuitive abilities. Trust in yourself, as well as trust in the origin of the information being given. Building a relationship with your Guides is key to this process. They are the interpreters of the vast sea of information that is available, and they will know how to filter what is in your highest interest to receive.

The following technique is called the "brain bypass." It will help you learn how to retrain your brain and build new pathways to receive intuitive information from your guides. The only rule is to trust yourself, and don't try to figure the information out in the beginning. Information from the other side is highly metaphoric and symbol based. If you try to "think" your way into understanding you will get caught in the web of confusion.

- Sit in a quiet space and take several deep breaths to prepare yourself to receive.
- Make the clear intention to connect to your personal Spirit Guides. If you like, you can ask for absolute protection and reaffirm that you are only willing to communicate with your God given guidance team. You are already in a space of light and love however, confirming this is always good if it adds to your feelings of security.
- The next step is to ask your Guides to show you "something." This may come in the form of a thought that passes into your mind rather than a clear image. Your Guides can show you any random thing under the sun, from numbers, animals, cartoons, street signs, symbols, memories, to the state of Texas. It doesn't matter what pops into your head, you just need to affirm the thing that is coming.

- We are not asking for any divine guidance or direction, we are just asking for a "random something." It is an important part of this process to note and affirm what is popping into your head. For example, if you see or have the thought of a kangaroo, say to your Guides, "Thank-you, I got your message of a kangaroo," and move on to the next thought or image.
- Your job is to catch and release. Don't try to make sense of anything at this point. You are only working on learning to receive beyond what your brain understands.

Holding the space for this practice is not always easy. Your guides communicate electrically, and you may not love the idea of sitting still and waiting for tiny thunderbolts in the form of silly information. However, this exercise is a powerful technique to restore your ability to receive.

After a week of asking for "something," you can gradually move into asking your Guides real questions. Don't try to figure it out, just receive! I will explain how to decipher your Guide's messages later in the book.

The Unexpected: Naturally Unnatural Events Rock Bottom: A Cellular Meltdown

Our biggest fear about our soul's contract is when we feel that we are headed for a painful situation. We avoid pain like the black plague. Sometimes it can be worse when situations arise that we didn't see coming, sending us down a spiraling rabbit hole without warning. Bad things happen to good people every day and it leaves us feeling helpless at the hands of fate.

Rock bottom is often referred to as "the dark night of the soul" for a reason. You feel like you are on lockdown in someone's cellar with no plan to escape. These shadowy valleys are not a punishment, but a death before a birth. Think for a moment about the process of transformation—the caterpillar is the perfect example. Biologists inform us that when a caterpillar is in the cocoon unable to move it is then when its cells are liquefying and turning to mush. There is a complete cellular meltdown. New cells that have been waiting for their chance to come on stage are activated by the death of the old cells. Biologists refer to the new cells as "Imaginal Cells." These are the cells of rebirth and create the miracle we know as the butterfly.

I truly believe that this activation by death occurs in human beings to some degree as well. Our states of depression and sadness place us in a cocoon where we await our transformation. This almost sounds downright exciting, except when you are the one in the thick of the experience. If only we could remember as the walls are closing in that this is a miracle in progress. This life changing transition occurs when we sink deeper into our cocoon of the endless moment.

How do we begin to dig out from our rock bottom and crack open our cocoon?

The antidote to dark is light. Light can draw you back into the land of the living, but it has been my experience that you can't tell a deeply depressed person to put on their happy face, open their dark shades and go smell the roses. This will land you the middle finger in most cases. Light can only seep through the keyhole opening that we are willing to provide. It is a step-by-step process of accepting love and raising your frequency. Opportunities will arise for a new life with every ladder rung you climb towards the light.

The Story of Sam: Rock Bottom Recovery

Sam came to me as a last resort. He proclaimed that he had absolutely nothing to live for and that his life was at rock bottom. Sam was recently divorced and employed as a truck driver. He spoke for thirty minutes about how everyone had wronged him over the course of his life. He told me that all he ever wanted to do was just be a decent God-fearing person.

Sam even told me that there was probably nothing I could do to help him and he wandered why he was even throwing his money away on a session.

I told Sam that maybe he was right, but since he was already here, we might as well see what we could do. I explained to him that it was imperative that he begin to raise his frequency to get out of the predicament that he was in. I told Sam that the way you raise your frequency is to find beauty and love that is already present in your life, and then begin fully focusing on that to solicit change and get back on track.

Sam did not drink my Kool-Aid.

He was annoyed and wanted to leave. I tried again. I told Sam that I wanted to ask some simple questions about his life before he left. The first question I threw out was "Do you like anything or anyone in your life at this time?" Sam, took a deep breath, and after a moment he mumbled "yeah, my dog." I asked Sam several questions about his dog and he seemed to become much lighter around this topic.

"This is the beginning of an opening," I told him. I sent Sam home with some experimental homework to find three things that he didn't despise about his life, and report back in a week.

To my surprise, Sam did exactly that! I saw him the following week and he was lighter in energy than the session before. He proudly listed off his three things and even "one to grow on."

1. His favorite show was renewed and back on for another season.
2. His favorite beer was now on tap at his frequently visited bar.
3. He lost 3 pounds.
4. He thought he lost his keys at Sam's Club, but he didn't; they were in a shopping bag.

We talked about his recent finds of lightness in his life and agreed that he should keep up this task. Once again, Sam came back exactly one week later and shared more evidence of light in his life. After a month of sessions, Sam was excited to share something wonderful that happened to him. His Ex-brother-in-law called him up to see if he would be willing to help him out in his motorcycle shop. Sam talked for thirty minutes straight on how much he used to "love" his motorcycle and spending weekends all greased up working on it. He was almost giddy, that he was going to get back into something he loved.

I asked Him why he didn't talk about motorcycles the first session we met if he loved them so much. Sam said, "Well I forgot how to love anything it didn't even come to my mind."

Sam could find the smallest openings for light in the darkest of hours and attracted a new life. All we need is a keyhole of positive presence in our life to focus on for our frequency to shift. One step at a time is the game plan for emerging from rock bottom.

Pain Gets a Job and a New Identity: Conversations with Goliath

I was in a troubled place when my guides lead me to do the "pain guide" process. I left the house early one morning to go to work and my car only made it as far as the local state park. I was feeling sick to my stomach with stress, so I canceled the work I had that day and just sat by the river. My body began to heat up like I had a fever, but I knew this feeling all too well. These were the physical symptoms that would come over me right before I am going in to a deep meditation to communicate with my guides.

I was told that "I had allowed fear to go too far in my mind and body and that if I didn't release it soon, I would become physically sick and fall into a well of darkness." Due to my sensitivity as a psychic,

I have always had to work hard to keep anxiety and outside energies at bay. This time was different than the others. I had already tried all my normal protocols for releasing my fear and anxieties, but nothing was touching this monster.

All I could do was pray to God and wait for the answer to come.

I continued to heat up and hear the familiar internal voices lead me through a process to confront my fears. I was told to see my fear and pain take on the form of a benevolent and loving being. It took me a moment to comprehend what I was being asked to do, when something seemed to be moving next to me along the riverside. I could feel my pain and fear expanding and mutating as if it was bubbling up and trying to leave my body to take on its own identity outside of me. I remained still as this meditation unfolded.

In moments, I was seeing what looked like a giant. I thought to myself "of course my pain and fear would manifest as a stinking giant!" I asked this gentle creature its name and he replied "Goliath. "Again, I thought, well of course it is, what else would you call a giant? I did my best to stay the course, even though the experience was turning out to be weirder than even my normal level of weird. I was told that I could ask my pain to guide any questions that I would like to better understand its purpose in my life. This internal mystical creature sat patiently while I decided if this experience I was having was real or not. I ultimately decided that I was desperate, and if this was the formula for happiness who am I to question God.

I began opening my heart and mind as tears streamed down my face. I began begging for answers as to why I had to hold this emotional war inside myself when I have already done so much work to release it. Slowly, I started to write words on my paper even though most of what was coming out seemed nonsensical. I wrote without regard to sounding eloquent or even sane. Words poured out, and it seemed that I was writing answers faster than I could ask the questions. I knew this was real. I could feel the presence of angels guiding and protecting this process.

Six hours had passed during this process. It felt like ten minutes! When it ended, I felt exhausted and limp from head to toe. Dazed, I picked up my belongings and walked back to my car. I wondered if I had just managed to perform a self-exorcism. I couldn't believe how much lighter and more peaceful I felt.

I am incredibly excited to share this process with you. For me, it was life changing. I no longer felt powerless in the face of my biggest fears. They finally have a loving place to go when I am unsuccessful at willing them away. Goliath thrives still and protects me from collapsing under the weight of my accumulated struggles. I giggle to myself when I think of my hungry giant, I just throw him a fear or two to satisfy his hunger! How would you like to hand off all that is ailing you? It is time to make your fear, anger and pain work hard and earn what life force and energy it has absorbed from your spirit.

Here's how to do it!

- This works best if you can go outside and find a quiet place in nature. If not, no problem; any quiet corner will do. Have a pen and paper ready to write down what comes to you.
- State your intention. I am ready to release the pain, anger, and shame that binds me. I am ready to release this from my identity so that it no longer holds me back, not one more single day. Please God, Guides, and Angels lead me back to a place where I am my lightest self.
- Warm up your imagination. (using the "catch and release" technique is an excellent warm-up for this active meditation)
- Remember, your imagination is just the gateway to your intuition, so don't keep it on a leash!

- Begin by allowing your eyes and vision to soften as if you were trying to see the aura of a tree through the slit of your eyes. Take several deep breaths here.
- Now allow your mind to wonder off and "imagine" that all your pain and problems were beginning to take a form. This form is a benevolent kind and loving being that is honored to hold and become an embodiment of what you wish to release. Take your time and allow your "Pain Guide" to manifest.
- Write down or affirm what you are seeing or thinking of as a loving being that holds your pain. Are they young or old? Male or female? Tall or short? Are there any names that come to you? This may take a little while, as you are most likely not used to using your intuitive imagination as an adult. Don't give up! Trust the things that are coming into your mind. Feel the love and kindness that radiates from this being that comes to you in service.
- Once you have an idea of what identity your pain has chosen to take. Begin by asking it any and every question that would help you

understand why you have experienced the pain and hardships that you have had in your lifetime. Purge your feelings and release your "whys."

- After you have asked a question, pick up your pen, and prepare to write down answers. Breathe deeply and don't think about if the answer is making sense, just write the first words that pop into your mind. Repeat this question and answer process until you feel a completion, or a good stopping point.

Chapter 5:

Decoding the Past: Learning to Fly Means Forgetting How to Fall

Dead Zone

My work as a medium has given me an insider's view of the true casualties of life. It is heartbreaking when an earthbound spirit is held back and believes that they can't move forward. In these cases, it is evident that the person has had a fear plagued life, or experiences so unsettling that they are unwilling or unable to cross over. Through investigations of countless old buildings and homes, I have been met with many spirits who were scared and angry about the way their life was handled when they were alive. Some of these spirits are heavy with regrets and guilt, while others seemed to be angry and caught up on a personal story of injustice.

When I am asked how this is even possible for a soul to become stuck if they have a divine plan and spirit guides I can only offer up the answer of "free will."

We all have free will. We can use this will to fly higher or fall deeper down in the hole. Heaven is a dimension of light- not only luminescent light as we think of it, but also light as in a "gravitational absence." The heavier a spirit is the more space between them and the lightness of the Heavenly realms.

Lizards and Smoke

I accompanied a team of paranormal experts to the house of a man and his family who were experiencing extreme paranormal activity. The man would come home from work to find pictures off the wall and water running. His children were frightened, as they reported seeing mist hang in their bedrooms at night and often would wake up with strange scratches. The man told the paranormal team that he thought this may be the spirit of his deceased "crazy ex-wife" haunting his home. When I began my walk through of this house I did not find a crazy ex-wife, but instead the spirit of an elderly woman who quickly started to speak and show me images about all that was upsetting her. According to her, she was the first owner of the house where she lived for many years and cared for her husband until he died. She showed me the room where she took care of him as he stayed bed ridden. The old woman seemed beside herself as she indicated her frustration about the new construction and remodeling that was underway in "her house"

The man who was now living in the house with his family was a contractor, and had recently gutted the old home and updated it. The woman went on frantically showing me images of her once clean home, freshly pressed laundry, blue floral macramé wall paper, and groomed rose bushes. As I looked around the house in its current state, I couldn't help but notice the piles of dirty laundry and clutter filled rooms. This alternative use of "her" house and different standards of cleanliness seemed to be what had the old woman so upset. As I was wrapping up my walk through I passed through a breezeway and the woman began yelling again, breaking into an angry chant "Lizards and smoke!" "Lizards and smoke!!" "Lizards and smoke!"

When I returned to the living room, I related my findings back to the team and to the man living in the house. He confirmed all the new house changes she was referring too and that he removed all the rose bushes shortly after purchasing the home. The only thing that didn't make sense was her angry chant. I asked the man if he understood

"Lizards and smoke." He didn't say a word, he just turned to the hallway, pulled open the accordion door to the laundry room where he revealed several tanks with iguana and lizard occupants. The man also confirmed that he did smoke, but only in his room. His room happened to be the same room where a wife cared for her husband until the day he died. The paranormal team did an incredible and professional job as they worked through the night in hopes to understand the stories of the spirit, and help bring closure to both sides.

After the investigation, the family reported that the paranormal activity had all but stopped. I feel in my heart that the team of people that came willing to hear this woman's story and frustrations, allowed her to release the pain she was holding and move on to the next phase of life in the afterlife.

Forgetting How to Fall - breaking out of the cycle

These are examples of extreme situations where a soul in the afterlife can become paralyzed from guilt, fear, or anger and heaviness is winning the battle. This experience of light and heavy is not only present in the afterlife, but also among the living. Our greatest universal rule is "like attracts like." Pain breeds more pain and happiness attracts more happiness. The heavier a soul becomes the more it is a magnet to attract dense heavy energy, making it difficult to return to the light. Without an intervention, this energy will just continue to create more of the same. This will result in an avalanche of imbalance.

We all carry our fair share of baggage from our lives, some more than others. Our eyes have seen tragedy, our ears have captured hateful words, and our hearts have felt the gravity of the world. Pain breaks us down, weakness sets in and then our brittle state believes the fear and anger that is talking to us inside our head. This is a vicious cycle that varies in degrees and longevity over the course of our lifetime. We need a divine intervention to lighten our load and stop this cycle.

Letting go of all that no longer serves us is the first step. This is forgiveness in a nutshell. This is easy enough to understand why we should do it, but doing it is a whole other ball game. Your fear and pain need to find justice in your heart not just in your brain. These traumas to your spirit have been on lockdown in your body and mind for possibly years and have now officially become a part of your identity. It will not die in vain.

Borrowed Wings

We all have heard the therapeutic term co-dependent and know that it is a state when a person can't be ok unless another person is ok first. Codependence is a common experience for someone who is sensitive or intuitive. They try to avoid confrontation at all costs. Empathic people will let their wants and needs fall to the way side as they sustain a muted life force in the form of other people's happiness. The essence of this energetic cycle is like living with borrowed wings. You can only fly if it doesn't cost anyone anything, so it is easier just to manage the ground and fly if it is someone else's idea first.

Because the energy exchange within an opposition is so painful for someone who is open and intuitive, it comes with a great cost to stand their ground. Empathic people can feel the fiery intent behind word missiles aimed at them. This fear of conflict usually begins in early years as children, when we were open and highly intuitive all the time. We had to learn how to survive and not capsize within the pain of these harsh circumstances and feelings, thereby learning to borrow wings to keep the peace as our own wings laid still and atrophied. Codependency is just another word to convey a cycle of energetic imbalance. Intuition and life force piggyback each other.

Life force is the breath in our body, and the God light we use to sustain life on Earth. When we give this energy away faster than we can fill it up, it keeps us in a cycle of failure to launch. Think of it like oxygen masks on an airplane. The stewardess always instructs you to put on your mask first in the case of an emergency, so that you can help those around you. It is not a selfish act to secure your own life force before others. It is just the makings of a win-win situation.

A larger part of regaining access to our natural intuition is beginning to recognize that we can always fly on our own. We don't need to wait for others to catch up or have the first idea of flight. Life force can come from an endless supply of support, you just need to know where to look for it.

Many gain access to this fountain of energy by way of meditation. When you are in a meditative state, you are opening yourself up to become recharged and plugged in to your intuition. There are many roads of meditation that will take you home and the only roadblock to this invaluable process is you getting in your own way.

People shudder when I suggest meditation to them as a means to return to their natural intuitive state. They quickly respond with "I can't meditate. I've tried and my brain won't shut up." The chattering of the mind is something people have spent years trying to overcome and still will tell you that, although it's better than when they started, they have yet to achieve perfect mental stillness.

We live in a very loud world with an equally loud ego consciousness. To find stillness and regain our life force we need to work on a different frequency. We need to go higher and leave the mental chaos far behind us.

Here is a fast and effective way to raise your frequency in a pinch!

Raising your Frequency

Energy follows your intent. It is a game of follow the leader. Try not to over complicate this technique. Your intention is enough to set you free.

- Begin by closing your eyes and taking a deep breath to clear the stage. State the intention of going to the highest frequency possible.
- Imagine for a moment a vehicle that will carry you up to the highest frequency. Anything from elevators to hot air balloons, whatever comes to you is perfect. If you can't seem to hold onto a vision of this, don't worry. The visual is not what is important, it is your intention that gets you where you want to go.
- Now take another deep breath and prepare to go up. With each breath, see yourself being effortlessly lifted. Count from

1 to 10 with each number you continue to float higher and higher. You may feel everything around you is growing brighter as you ascend to the top. Keep breathing and counting until you reach the number ten.

- Finally, when you are at the top, open your eyes quickly and notice how you are feeling. Are you lighter? Is the room around you blurry? Is there a tingling in your body? Note anything that seems to be different than when you started. Notice how your mind chatter is not as loud as it was just a few moments ago.
- You have arrived at your destination, a higher frequency!

Even if you are not wowed by the shift, your energy is still playing "follow the leader" and complied as it followed you up the magic beanstalk. Practice this every day, thirty seconds to a minute to refill your life force bucket.

The more you know the more you grow

Messages from the other side are often given in the formula of an encrypted metaphor. Although it may feel like it, our Guides don't deliver messages in this fashion simply to watch us lose our mind and temper while bamboozling us at the game of life. There is an actual purpose to their creative chaos. Each symbol that is sent to you from your Guides is loaded with volumes of information. So much information, that it would take hours to explain if you were to just sit down and discuss it over a cup of tea. Every piece of information is a building block for the next. Your Guides speak a vertical language. If you are trying to listen for full sentences, you may discover that the conclusion of the messages never come. Your answers are not at the end of a sentence, they are under the sentence!

Gifted Instead of Broken

One day I had a new client stroll through my door. She was a poster woman for a kind and loving soul. This was going to be her first reading and she was beyond excited. The first image that came to me as I tuned in to this woman was a "dolphin." I thought it was a strange message, but I know never to throw anything away. I set the message aside and waited for the next piece of information to float into my mind. Within seconds, I heard the word "teacher." I asked the woman if she was a teacher and she energetically confirmed that she was, and asked how I could possibly know that. I couldn't help but smile and let out a laugh. The teacher joined the laughter as she said "oh yeah! I guess that's the point. You're a psychic." The next image that came through was in the shape of a puzzle piece. Silently in my head, I asked my Guides what that meant, and I heard "what does it mean to you?" Before I could even take a moment to consider what that symbol meant, I had a flash of insight that this was the symbol for autism. I asked the teacher if she taught autistic children. The teacher eagerly confirmed this as well. The dolphin then came back into my mind flashing at me like traffic light.

I took a moment to consider what dolphins represented to me, and I concluded that it was their high intelligence and abilities to connect telepathically that stood out. All at once, the cryptic message came together for me. I asked the teacher if she felt stunted in her career, because she saw these autistic children as highly intelligent and telepathically gifted instead of behind the curve and handicapped. I told her that I felt she had no one to confide in for fear of looking crazy or unprofessional. The teacher looked at me as big tears began to stream down her face. She confirmed this, and continued to share how saddened she was to see highly evolved souls able to communicate in a language beyond words in an educational system that wanted no part of her theory. She saw the children as gifted instead of broken.

As we receive symbols in the form of message from our Guides, we begin to familiarize ourselves with their meanings. After that reading, I now know if I see dolphin, that it represents intelligence and telepathy. I have over the years come to understand many of my guides' personal symbols and signs. It is an interdimensional short hand. Each symbol builds on the next as you deepen and ask "what does this mean to me?" Begin by building your own personal symbol dictionary. Each time you see a symbol record it and its meaning. It is just like learning another language!

I am still in awe how a whole story can be told with just a handful of visual clues. I can't imagine how, with words alone, one could explain the emotions of a teacher and her beliefs about children with unseen potential. This beautiful language will continue to grow the more symbols you know. It is our job to dig deeper and find the true meaning.

Our Natural Order

When opening to access your intuition there is a great importance in working to remove anything that would block the natural flow of your intuitive processes. We are born with our heavenly communicators in pristine condition. We don't lose our sensitive intuition; we block it for survival purposes. Our "ego" is often the block and captor of this bird we wish to set free. Pride and judgment are constrictions that keep us from opening to the bounty intuition has to offer our life. The more sensitive and gifted with intuitive abilities you are the greater the struggle can be.

Intuition requires you to feel more than your own feelings, know more than your own thoughts, and see and hear energetic expression outside of your own. All while holding onto the belief that your experiencing psychic exchanges. The stakes are high to keep this ability intact, but worth it. The good news is that the world is changing, and this evolutionary shift is taking us back to our natural order and beyond. The transformation the Earth is going through will require us to make the transition back to our sensitive nature to survive and thrive in the intuitive age. We are training to become warriors of powerful sensitivity, and live with an open heart and open mind. Remember, you are only looking to take back what is already yours to have. Intuitive communication is your birthright.

Wordless: Intuitive Communication

In the psychic world, we refer to something called the "four clairs" as a way someone receives intuitive information. You can think of them as your own personal input output AV ports, like on your television set and DVD player. The first is "claircognizance," intuitive information that comes in the form of "thoughts." The second is "clairvoyance," intuitive information that comes to you as an image or vision in your mind. Third is "clairaudience," intuitive information that comes in the form of words or sentences in your own voice, and in your own mind. Lastly, there is "clairsentience," intuitive information that is felt in the body.

Claircognizance

All of these intuitive ports are linked to the energy centers inside of your body mind and spirit. Claircognizance, is connected to the crown chakra located at the top of your head. This information can be one of the more difficult ones to detect and separate from our own everyday thoughts. Intuitive thoughts that come through this portal will feel like your own thought, in your own voice—but with a subtle twist. This type of information usually interrupts your "normal" everyday hamster wheel mind, and feels like someone threw a life preserver that plopped right down in the middle of the sea of your thoughts. These thoughts have a plum line effect. You can be on chatterbox mode inside of your mind, and then all of a sudden, plop! A thought that told you to "turn left to avoid construction work." Or, plop! A thought that tells you that "your child forgot their homework." Plop! "You're going to get a promotion." These thoughts are the calm voice inside of our monkey mind, that definitely make a splash if you are tuned into your intuition.

Spirit Guides will frequently communicate to you through claircognizance. It is not uncommon to feel like there are small electrical pops on the top of your head, or feelings of tightness from expansion when this chakra is being used for communication. We have blocked this natural energy portal by overuse of our small thinking and analytical processes. When we feel that we need to figure out the answers, we can contract and shut down this energy center blocking us from accessing information from a broader more expansive view.

When opening back up to the use of your claircognizance ability, try the simple meditation practice of imagining the top of your head opening. Imagine a sunroof as you hit the button and roll back the top to let the light in. Just sit and bask in the light with no expectations other than just receiving love and light to refill your energy tank. You can also switch it up by imagining your crown as a flower opening from a bud to full bloom and drinking in the sun. Claircognizance can be one of your strongest bridges to the other side, if you are willing to leave your mental box and open your mind to the journey of endless possibilities.

Clairvoyance

Clairvoyance is the most popular of all the extra sensory abilities and is connecting to the "third eye" chakra. For centuries, many cultures have revered their clairvoyants, seers, oracles, and prophets as spiritual beings who are able to see and receive information from beyond the veil. Beginners tend to put the most pressure on this experience of second sight, as it seems to reside on an intuitive pedestal. Most people want to "see it to believe it." However, if you don't know what you are looking for, or if you're expecting too much you may miss it!

The truth is, inner sight is a natural communication skill we use in some form every single day. If you are daydreaming or night dreaming, you are using your clairvoyant faculties. People I have worked with to open this ability often get frustrated and stuck because they are expecting a bright three-dimensional movie to unfold. Not to say that the movie version never happens, it is just more likely to be the grand finale desert, rather than the meat and potatoes of everyday clairvoyant experiences.

Try this to test your inner sight:

- Close your eyes and begin to "think" about your kitchen.
- Walk over to the refrigerator and open the door and close it.

- Now, walk over to your kitchen table and pull out all the chairs and then put them all back.
- Finally, look at the clock nearest your kitchen, see what time it is on the clock and say the numbers of the time out loud.

Believe it or not, that experience was you being able to use your inner sight! It feels more like you are recalling a memory than a multidimensional firework show. Guides will send messages in the form of symbols and signs to your inner sight. These clairvoyant visions come into inner sight in a subdued manner. If you are expecting too much you may miss the message.

- To strengthen this ability, write a list of random objects on a piece of paper.
- Go down the list visualizing each object, and then visualize each object deconstructing. For example, see a rose in your mind's eye and watch each pedal fall off and crumble. See a chair and watch the weather beat it down slowly until it is a pile

of splinters. This visual exercise will help you hold the third eye chakra open and build the muscle.

Another technique for developing this intuitive connector, is to visualize an eye. Notice if the eye can stay open, or if it is half closed. Sometimes the eye comes through in a cloudy haze. Just keep trying, you will build this inner sight the more you flex your clairvoyant muscles.

Clairaudience

Clairaudience connects to the throat chakra and it is the way we experience inner hearing. A good example of clairaudience is when a song gets stuck in our head. We hum along to the tune in our mind until we catch ourselves and make the random announcement"I have a song stuck in my head." Only then, when you notice the monotonous lyrics, does it seem to leave your mental karaoke. It did its job: it got your attention! Songs stuck in the head are almost always a sure sign from your Guides or loved ones up above. They often will leave messages on loop to get their point across. The next time this happens to you, listen closely to the lyrics of the song. Ask yourself what they mean to you and recognize if this song connects you with any memory or past time.

I remember as a child on a regular basis I would hear someone calling by name, especially while I was going in or out of sleep. If you have ever had this happen to you, then you know the frightful yet exciting feeling of hearing an anonymous exterior voice inside of your own head. It is definitely an experience you never forget.

Sound seems to be one of the easier conductors of energy from the other side. Similar to clairvoyance, clairaudience comes in as subtle spurts of information in the form of a handful of words. We can pick up on this type of telecommunication from the living as well as the other side. Have you ever "heard" what your spouse or friend is thinking? Or one or two words pop into your head as you pass by a stranger? If this happens, then you have experienced clairaudient communication and are not far from developing your interdimensional listening skills.

Clairsentience

Clairsentience is the ability of intuitive feeling and is connected to all the chakras. People who are highly sensitive to energy are called empaths. An empath can often have a difficult time discerning which emotions are theirs and which emotions belong to other people. Unaware empaths can have a severe struggle in life, as they experience all feelings as their own and are drawn to other peoples' pain with little to no insight from seeing, hearing, or knowledge from the other intuitive receivers. This ability can become overwhelming, due to its monopoly over the chakras system. These empathic individuals are the wallflowers of our society and can work to develop this gift to become natural intuitive healers and doctors of the future.

Clairsentience is to blame when we have those "gut" feelings. This ability partners well with Claircognizance, the feeling and the knowing can make for powerful life directors. The gift of feeling is often not experienced as a gift, but a curse. However, it can also be one of the deepest ways we can experience life and interface with the other side. When we are moved by a strong emotion this is when our heart and mind are widely open to receiving. The journey of clairsentience is finding the core of who you are and your own personal emotional set point so that you can "be in this world but not of it."

The Power of Perception

The way we perceive life counts for everything. Perception determines your souls experience over the course of your life. Seeing the other side is just a matter of tweaking and expanding your perception of what is possible. Your beliefs about what is real are the headlights scouring the road ahead of you. You will see only what you are willing to see. If you have trained yourself to seek out potential danger or miss happenings, you will begin to see this layer of life. If you are focused on finding the keyholes of opportunity, again this is where your perception will lead you.

We do the best we can to see the glass half full and make lemonade with our lemons but underneath some of our best attempts our fears can take over. It is much easier said than done. The foundation of our inner child holds the key to resetting some of our internal switches. Our attempts to transcend can be thwarted if we don't follow the road back to the beginning of our beliefs. We begin to build our foundation for our future by answering one simple question: Which team are you on? Team A or team B.

Team A believes that everything has a reason and a purpose and that there are no accidents. They believe magic and miracles are real. This team also believes that you are always divinely supported and guided even in times of trial. Team B believes that this world is every man and woman for themselves and you need to be on the lookout for danger and deceit at all times to protect yourself. This team also believes life is full of random experiences around every corner and that the other shoe may drop at any moment.

This may seem like a harsh division but they are opposing beliefs. One of these perceptions is inlaid to the core of who you are. There actually is no right and wrong within this suggestion of teams, it is just two different paths of perception. There is always a choice. The easier road sets you off with the belief of universal backing and events within divine order. Even though you don't like a current situation, you choose not to struggle and fight things that are out of your control. You give way to the understanding that unwanted life events have a higher purpose, even if you can't understand it. There is peace in the pain within this perception of life. Alternatively, the hard road is earned with every breath while fighting to safe guard yourself against all potential threats. It leaves you refusing to really trust anyone while never laying down the fight and pain- no matter how much your hands are tied. This road has built its identity on the unfortunate unfoldings of life.

We all know that we would prefer the easier road over the harder one but is that the belief you would find at the core of who you are? Does your inner child know how to find easy street? Our life had molded us into the person we are today but it is never too late to go back and change your reality settings.

How to Reset Your Settings

The subconscious holds your fears deep in the vault of your being. We need to take a journey back in time to release all beliefs that no longer serve you.

• Begin by lying down and imagining that you are walking down the side of a highway and each mile marker you come across represents a memory from your past that has stuck with you and lead you to believe in the harsher side of life.

• Ask that the best of the situation join you on your journey as a ball of light emerges from the hardship you are facing. If you are seeing a child version of yourself, reach out your hand and ask the child to walk with you.

• Keep walking down this road stopping at each memory mile marker and recovering the light while leaving the rest.

• As you feel you are approaching the end of the road, imagine that you see a vault sitting right in the middle of the highway. This is the closet that holds your deepest skeletons.

• Call on your Guides to be present as you slowly open the door to your vault. Trust what you see and resist any urge to change it.

• Take all the light and recovered strength you have found and use it to make a ball of light ten times bigger than you.

• Once you feel ready, place this light around everything in this vault and dissolve it all the way away until it is just a pile of ashes on the ground.

• All the light and children have been returned to their rightful owner. Take a moment to set new intentions for your belief settings allowing your heart to open as fears resign as your captor and leave your body, allowing white light to fill its place.

As you move forward in life, actively look ahead of yourself for opportunities to capture evidence of light. If you come across someone or something that you don't like, try and find five things that you do like about that person or situation and then bless them and send them on their way!

The Surrender Story

Letting go and allowing our destiny to unfold and our soul's growth to take place is one of the hardest things for us as humans to do. To manifest our dreams into reality the best plan of action is to draw our desires into the openness of our conscience wanting and then release it to the higher universal forum to be created outside of our limited thinking. We generally want a hand in this creative process to better control the outcome. Most of the time when we think we have let something go and given it to God we really have not yet met the depths of a true surrender. Surrendering is not just one swift action but a series of events helping you to let go more and more until you finally release it entirely. The story I am about to share with you may be hard to believe, but it is the absolute truth, and the strangest thing that I have ever experienced to this day.

One late night years ago in the height of my psychic studies, I awoke to find myself standing in my basement. I was perplexed because I didn't remember walking down stairs, but what was even more shocking was when three spirits appeared in front of me in my basement. One spirit looked like a Native American Indian, the second was in the form of a tiny Asian woman, and the third never really took any form that I could recognize. It was just a shapeless energy. The Indian never moved his lips but communicated with me telepathically. He said that he was there to teach me how to "let go." I knew somehow that he was referring to my ongoing psychic research and training.

I had read every book I could get my hands on but my intuitive ability still seemed to be rogue and un-tempered. The intuitive information I was accessing was becoming increasingly overwhelming as it was coming in. Paralyzed by this odd encounter I couldn't do anything but stare at these three beings. The Indian instructed me to watch him as he was going to show me how to "let go." Within a split second, there was a bright ball of light in front of the Indian similar to a camera flash. He followed the bright light by saying "now you do it."

I knew they wanted me to "let go" but I had utterly no idea or instructions on how to perform this task, much less create a ball of light to appear. I closed my eyes and took a deep breath still pulsing with adrenaline over my newly found friend status and tried to relax and just "let go." After a few breaths, I opened my eyes to see the three spirits still standing and watching. The Indian spoke again with a perfect tone and no emotional inflection as he said" you didn't do it." The Asian woman lead me through the same process, and one again I was told "you didn't do it." This cycle of this exchange went on back and forth for some time. I am not sure how much time passed during this experience. It could have been 5 minutes or 5 hours I was so scared and excited that I lost all concept of time.

Finally, this twilight zone came to an end as the Indian instructed me to let go once again. I closed my eyes and felt full of frustration by my continuing failure, I didn't even bother trying to let go. I opened my eyes one last time as I heard the words "you didn't do it" I began yelling at them telling them "I can't, and that if this is what it takes to hone your psychic talents, then I give up!" Just as soon as I proclaimed my psychic retirement a bright ball of light appeared in front of my head like a camera flash and then promptly disappeared. I looked at the Indian and he simply stated, "you did it" as they all disappeared.

It took me several months to figure out what in the world I had achieved that night. Ultimately, I realized that it was all done for my personal lesson in surrendering. I had wanted to develop my gifts so much that I was getting in my own way and constricting the possibilities. My willingness to completely give up and release my dreams, was the very thing that advanced it.

Just when you think you have let go and let God take over, you probably still have layers left to your letting go process. If you become stuck in the advancement of your intuitive pursuits or any life goals, sometimes the adventure unfolds by way of a beautiful surrender.

Learning to let go and let God when you desperately want something is the most effective way to get exactly what you want.

Chapter 6

Patterns of the Present: Symbols and Synchronicity

Learning to be Present

If you have ever attempted to meditate then you probably know how such a simple process of being present in the moment can be one of the most difficult things to do. There are innumerable resources and practitioners out there to help guide you on your meditation practice, but the journey must begin with the first step-presence. All intuitive information is given to you in the "now moment." Most of us spend our mental energy trying to figure out our life. Everyday questions such as "What should I cook for dinner?" and "How am I going to get to a career that I love?" and "Where is my perfect partner, how will I meet them?"

If our mind is not found rambling through our future moments, it can be alternatively found hung up in our past. "I wish I never said those things to my child," or "I wish I had tried harder in school, so that I had more career opportunities," or "I wish I told my father I loved him more before he passed, "or "I wish I didn't eat that spicy Indian food last night." The majority of the day, especially if we have a moment of free time is spent thinking. Thinking, thinking and more thinking. We *think* ourselves to a point of exhaustion. This over the top analysis of life is quickly becoming a part of our outmoded existence. As we continue to evolve, our old thinking will become limited and slow, similar to the old dial up internet. Our new thoughts in the form of intuitive hits, will come in fast and clear like wireless high-speed internet.

Tapping into the fast lane of our thoughts means we learn to replace "thinking" with "knowing." To survive this upgrade, we must become completely comfortable with the present moment. Staying in the now can feel in the beginning like you are in a straightjacket and someone has locked you in a dark room. It is difficult, because it is foreign. It is not the way most of us have been taught to approach life. Learning to stay present is a process of catching yourself when your mind goes into wanderlust mode and bringing it back to what is happening in your moment of right now.

Your Spirit Guides communicate with you in the present moment. They cannot reach you in the mists of your past or future because, now is all we ever really have. We cannot relive our past in the present, nor can we embody a future that doesn't exist yet. We are right where we stand, for better or worse. The "knowing" comes to us when we have found enough grace in our spirit to hold the door open and let intuitive answers enter our mind. Your divine directors wait patiently each day to meet you in the present, and offer you the guidance you have been asking for.

The Sandwich Meditation

Several years ago, I ran across the beautiful work of Eckhart Tolle through his book "The Power of Now." I knew that learning to sustain life in the present moment was the next step to communicating deeper with my Spirit Guides.

I committed myself fully to the teachings of Eckhart Tolle and woke up each day determined to stay in the present moment. I would not allow myself to get distracted or pulled into daydreaming as I normally would. It can be exponentially more difficult for someone with a highly intuitive mind to stay present due to their ability to take in so much information all at once. It becomes a mental mosh-pit.

Despite my best efforts to stay in the now moment, I found that I couldn't hold that place more than a few minutes at a time. If anyone at work crossed my path and began to talk to me I would forget about my pledge to the present, and my mind would become absorbed in conversation, enviably circling back around my "to do" list. I don't give up easily. My attempts to stay focused solely on the present moment went on for weeks.

Defeat finally set in. The day I was ready to give up on this practice my guides held an intervention. On my way home from work I stopped to get my usual after work chicken sandwich, when a loud thought came crashing into my mind: "Be present with the sandwich" it said. Thinking that was a ridiculous idea, I preceded to unwrap my sandwich. Again, a booming internal voice echoed in my head: "Wait until you get home to eat. Be present with the sandwich." It was curiosity, not obedience, that made me decide to heed this strange advice.

Once I made it home I sat down at the kitchen table and slowly unwrapped my chicken sandwich. I took the first bite and slowed my chewing down to a snail's pace. The first thing I noticed was that the sesame seeds on the bun felt like furniture sliders on my molars. Next, was the indivisible chicken that felt and tasted like a discarded rubber tire. I continued my slow chewing for the better part of a minute, when I noticed some strange happenings. The first thing that revealed itself to me was that my longtime favorite sandwich was quite undesirable. The second thing that stood out in that moment of presence was my upgraded hearing. It seemed like there were hundreds of birds chirping at maximum volume outside of my kitchen window. I could hear the clock ticking three rooms over. If superman hearing wasn't enough, I began to see what looked like static electricity coursing through the air around me. I had reached the height of my freak-out meter. I dropped the sandwich and hightailed it out of the kitchen. My short lived super senses returned to normal as I stood at a safe distance from the kitchen, completely confused by my paranormal sandwich encounter.

Later that evening in meditation I began to understand what had unfolded for me that afternoon. I was clear now of exactly what it feels like when you slowdown and dig deep into the present moment. No wonder we run fast into our future. Awareness in the present moment stimulates our senses as they expand and boot up. It can be quite unsettling in the beginning, this may explain why so many people experience anxiety in absolute stillness and are resistant to meditation. The good news is that the beginning is only the beginning. After you make it past any initial shock of living in the now you can experience thought outside of the box and upgrade to intuitive living.

Your Sandwich Meditation Steps

The first step into your own experience of "the sandwich meditation" is to find something you do frequently on auto pilot. It doesn't have to be eating a sandwich. You could practice this technique while washing the dishes, walking the dog, grocery shopping or even exercising. Any monotonous semiconscious activity will do!

- Next, close your eyes and take a deep breath. Set the intention to slow down and dig deeper into your present moment.
- Open your eyes and slowly proceed with your task.
- Move slower and slower until your senses begin to heighten.
- Notice the details about your activity. If you are washing dishes, listen to the sound of the water, can you feel the vibration of its movement? Look at your dishes closely, can you see the brush stokes or scratches? Take note of the smallest details possible, and breathe deeply. If you are taking a walk in the park, try isolating different sounds. Listen only to the sound of children or birds. Let your eyes fall to the details of a park bench. What is etched in its wood? How many colors

can you see? The weirder the better when it comes to this meditation!

- Do this exercise no longer than 30 seconds to a minute.
- If you want to get better at staying in the now, try this more frequently throughout the day, not in longer intervals. You will retrain the pathways in your brain the more you practice slowing down and tuning into the magical moment of right now!

When I was 13, I channeled a poem about the spoils of focusing on the future and abandoning the present.

There is a Soul I Know

There is a soul I know that lives in the world to come. He sits in silencing thought throughout the days.

There are few that can follow him when he speaks his words of wisdom.

His faith remains in God, and all of the revelations to come; he knows there is a peace in such faith.

The motionless expression upon his face isn't one of ignorance, but one of the wise. His gray eyes reflect the feelings of our world today.

He speaks of the events to come, and their destruction. "The knowledge of the future comes from the Holy Nation from above; he proclaims.

There is a soul I know that lives in the world to come, a wise man that could tell your fate, but how shameful that such a wise man could be so foolish as to dwell on tomorrow while wasting today.

Changing Your Life Requires You to be a Co-Creator Operation: Believe

Remembering to ask and learning to receive are the two most valuable tools when building a working relationship with your Guides. The thought of inter dimensional beings watching over you to endorse your life and illuminate your path may feel strange in the beginning. This is to be expected. It is likely that this type of relationship has lived outside of your belief systems for most of your lifetime. This is a leap of faith. To see evidence of these benevolent helpers you need to begin with the first step: Believing. They will not come down and rescue you from the choices you have made. Your Guides are with you to assist you and your focus in taking your life to its fullest potential. This is a co-creative relationship. When you clear out a space and set the stage in your life for them to operate, the magic begins.

Setting the Stage for Co-Creation Lesson 1: "Thank you, more please."

The spirit guide world operates within the sacredness of life. There is nothing but love and pure intent driving this intelligence. To meet them half way we begin with gratitude. Gratitude is the fuel of life: it is the energetic speed setting of receiving. If we cannot find gratitude it will be almost impossible to recognize the gifts that we receive from the other side. Connecting to gratitude can sometimes invoke guilt and can put the brakes on receiving further abundance. Feeling guilty that we should be more grateful for all the beautiful blessings that life has bestowed doesn't truly allow your heart to lift and open to its full capacity.

Experiencing gratitude in it's pure form means that we have found balance in the present moment. Balance is feeling gratitude with honor both appreciating the gifts and believing that they are yours to have.

I watched a movie years ago that has stuck with me and has become a personal mantra. In the movie, an Indian cab driver is explaining the secrets of life to a young troubled woman. He tells her about the magic of "Thank you, more please." This is the perfect formula for keeping gratitude alive in your life and drawing in more of what makes you happy. It is the asking and the receiving all in one shot! I use this mantra dozens of times each day to show my appreciation for the divine gifts I receive, and affirm through gratitude that I will stay open to receive more.

"Thank you more please" are the universal magic words to open the door for God and your Guides to facilitate miracles in your life. To invoke large changes in your life, begin with the little things. Say a simple "Thank you more please" in response to a kind person who holds the elevator door open as you are rushing to your appointment. Or even recite it in response to beautiful day that makes you smile. This simple phrase has the alchemic ability to turn the gratitude for receiving a cup of coffee into the creation of open doors to your dreams. The next time that you spot a moment of wonderful in your life shout to the heavens: "Hallelujah! thank you, more please!" and watch the miracles line up at your door!

Soul Revival Lesson 2: Creating sacred space

Your energy management is important to maintain connections to your guidance team. Just like your car it will take you anywhere you want to go. But it is your job to fill up the tank with gasoline. Filling up your energy tank is a simple process that just requires a little dedication. To prepare, it is helpful to begin by setting up a sacred space in your home. It doesn't need to be an elaborate alter, just a small space that represents stillness and peace. It also helps to have articles that remind you of sacred connections such as stones, pictures, crosses or books. Colors of your liking also help bring you to a state of reception. This sacred space is your own personal launching pad. It is helpful to start each day in this space as you place your intentions for the upcoming day. I have often sat in my sacred space to set my intentions and catch myself affirming what I would refer to as "big intentions" and completely overlooking my smaller intentions. Such as, "please guide me to help save the world and make a difference in world peace", while disregarding my current need for focus and intentions on remaining peaceful while driving in rapturous traffic that day.

This space will give back exactly what you put into it. If you come baring your heart and soul you will receive more than counter proportions of love to fill up the tank that you so willingly opened. As you lay down your burdens and prepare to refill your heart with lightness, listen to your intuition as to where you should focus your energy that day. You may be surprised at the answers you receive.

On one of my off days, I was excited to go out for a solo all-day hike at the local state park. As any mother would tell you, "me" days are the holy grail of a mothers' existence! I had prepared the night before and packed all my water, food and maps so I could ensure an early start. I sat down for my morning meditation and daily intention setting and was almost too excited about my hike to get to sacred space and bare my soul. Once I finished reviewing all that I was grateful for and setting intentions for my day. I allowed my mind to go soft and aimless as I surfed the quiet connection to my guides, remaining open to receive any additional messages. What came to me was quite unexpected. My thought messages kept coming in and advising me to stay home and rest instead of going hiking. This was odd information. I asked my Guides if I was in danger by hiking and I received a firm "no." I came out of my meditation with a burst bubble. I decided to go hiking anyway, but to just keep it at an easy pace. Two hours into my hike, I began to feel dizzy and feverish with a side of nausea. I thought it must be that 24-hour flu going around. I sat down to eat a snack. My energy was draining fast and I felt weak as a kitten. I didn't really know if I could find the strength to turn around and make the long hike back to my car.

With no cell phone reception, I was officially stuck between a rock and a hard place. I began putting all my intention and focused prayers into the strength to walk. The lyrics "Swing low sweet chariot, coming for to carry me home" came rushing into my head. I began to think of the strength it must have taken for the slaves to find their way to freedom. I remembered being fascinated with Harriet Tubman and the Underground Railroad when I was a child. I was in far better shape than those poor desperate souls. I began my hike back focusing on singing "swing low sweet chariot" repeatedly, all the way back to my car. I slept in my car for the next few hours before returning home.

The messages and lesson behind this experience is that it is always best to trust your first instinct and messages from your Guides. However, in the instance that you don't, they will always know the strategy to get you back home every time.

I know my Guides helped me to gain focus and strength through song and remembrance of the brave and strong that came before me.

Lesson 3: Creating Sacred Space Outside of Your Home

Setting the stage for conversation with your Guides is not only helpful with life direction, but it also can be downright fun! Your Guides will always follow your lead and meet you half way. Instead of waiting around for possible signs, it is entirely possible to create your own stage to receive messages within a 24-hour turn around. To be a co-creator with the other side, give your guides a job to do.

Ask them to give you a message with the next song that comes on the radio, or messages through opening a random book and reading the first paragraph that meets your eyes.

To set the stage, the first thing you want to do is close your eyes, take a deep breath and ask your own ego to step aside. Then through the power of intention state your request. For example, if you are worried about a family member and you don't know how to best help them, ask your Guides to help you see, know, feel or hear the answer to your request within the confines of your day. Pay attention to all possible portals such as social media posts, conversations with a friend and even overhearing conversations of strangers.

Your answer will come.

Your job is to stay present and receptive.

There have been many times I have asked for a very specific question to be answered within a movie I was getting ready to watch or through animal signs and even numbers on a receipt total. Setting the stage to receive has no limits, if you can dream up the stage, your guides can meet you there! Don't get discouraged if your answers do not come right away. This is a communication skill that takes practice. You are learning to tune in and trust messages in the form of life's subtleties. The more you practice the better you will become. Just ask and you shall receive!

Creating Forward Momentum with Your Intuition

As you begin to adapt to a new normal, and live an intuition driven lifestyle there are a few tactical tools that will ensure that you stay focused and moving forward!

Get Grounded

Grounding is the key to connecting Heaven to Earth. We are grounded when we are present in mind, body, and spirit. Intuitive experiences can sweep you off your feet and before you know it, you are hours invested within a daydream and checked out of reality. The trick is balancing both worlds. Grounding will help build the stamina you need to maintain your dual citizenship lifestyle. Before I give an intuitive reading, I always ground myself so I can make sense and order out of the esoteric information that is being given to me. There are many techniques to help with grounding, here are a few of my personal favorites:

Try this quick meditation before you start your day.

- Close your eyes and stand or sit with your feet firmly on the floor hip distance apart.
- State the intention to become grounded.
- Begin to feel like you are a tree and imagine your roots running from your hips down each one of your legs and into the floor.
- Your roots continue to grow deeper through each mantle of the earth's crust until you meet the center of the Earth.
- Imagine for a moment, that the center of the Earth is a bright glowing ball of light energy as you wrap your roots around it and anchor yourself.

- Feel the sensation of this bright center of the Earth energy then beginning to infiltrate your roots and slowly rising back up through the layers of the Earth, into your feet, up each of your legs and into the rest of your body.
- Let us rise all the way up until it reaches the top of your head.
- Open your eyes and feel what it feels like to be grounded. This will stay with you for a while.
- Check back in halfway through your day to see if you need to be re grounded and repeat this simple meditation of necessary.
- Another great tool to aid your grounding is stones. I keep simple river stones close to my bedside table to hold and ground at night, and a few in my purse to help me whenever I need quick grounding during the day.
- If you find yourself becoming chronically spacey, try eating smaller meals throughout the day to stay rooted in your body. Food is another way we ground

ourselves to the Earth and stay focused in our 3rd dimensional lives.

Clearing Your Space

If you are having trouble connecting to your Guides and intuition. Your space may be too dense and is holding you back like concrete shoes when you're trying to take off for flight. The energy around your physical body counts as much as the energy on the inside your body. Heavy space around you effects the way you interact with your Guides, as there must be a conducive vibrational meeting place to connect.

The environmental heavyweight may be coming from things, residual energy from situations or the people you live with. Don't worry about it if you do find that a spiritual cleanse is in order. Everyone encounters a need to clear their space from time to time; this is a common occurrence. If you feel yourself slipping into a bad mood or getting instantly tired when you enter your home or work environment these may be indicators that your space needs some energetic elbow grease to get it back to spic and span!

Here are some tools to use when clearing space.

Smudging is a good form of evicting lower vibrations from your space. It is done most commonly with a smudge stick that is made up of dried sage wrapped in a bundle. When smudging to clear space begin by closing your eyes and asking your Guides to help you release anything that does not serve you and your energy. Open your eyes and light the sage. A light stream of smoke will begin to emerge from the bundle. Simply walk around each corner of the room wafting the smoke and unwanted energy in the direction of the door or window. It is just like sweeping your kitchen. You sweep all the dirt into a pile, then into the dustpan where it receives its charter service into the trash can. This dissolves the disorder of any energy that has been disruptive to your intuitive practice and overall wellbeing.

Another way to clear your space is with the use of sound. Tuning forks and singing bowls emit sound waves that also have a curative effect on your personal energy as well as the surrounding environment.

Clearing Your Mind

We already know that we can get in our own way and become our worst enemy when it comes to drawing out the natural intuitive abilities. Our mind is complex and conditioned by our past experiences, keeping us trapped in the hamster wheel of our recycled thoughts and beliefs. Nothing short of a reset or override will set us in a new direction. Meditation is truly the shortest road to your inner worlds, even though in the beginning it can be turbulent within the mine field of our thoughts.

I have created a special meditation to help prep the overactive mind for meditation, and create a compartmentalization for your everyday thoughts. This meditation is called "The Backwards Meditation."

The Backwards Meditation Explained

Science tells us that the 95 percent of our thoughts are repetitive. That is shocking when you consider the lack of room left for new thought possibilities! This meditation is designed to split you in half so that your repetitive thoughts have their own hamster wheel and side of you, while the other side of you plays witness, and remains open for intuitive information. We are not looking to release thoughts like in most common meditative practices. We are doing the opposite with "backwards meditation." We are becoming scientists in lab coats, looking to draw thoughts closer for inspection!

Sit back, get comfortable and prepare to watch the movie of your thoughts! Close your eyes and imagine that you are sitting in a nice comfy chair eating popcorn in your personal home movie theatre. Everyone is off to school and work and it's you alone ready to watch the story of your thoughts. Some days your thoughts will cross the screen slowly, like clouds drifting through the sky. Other days your thoughts will look like a Chinese ping pong tournament. Your job in the room is to just notice and be a witness to the thoughts that come up and under no circumstances try to change them. Just notice the thought and label it with one or two words. Try to stay emotionally removed from the things that pop up in your mind or on your home movie theater screen. You are not the judge, just the witness. Take note of whatever thoughts pop into your head for 30 seconds to a minute.

For example, if your "to-do list" pops onto your internal screen, let it come in as you give it a one to two word label, such as "answer email," "oil change," or "dinner," even if your thoughts are all about answering emails for the entire time, just say. Email…email…. email...Like a metronome, your thoughts will come in and click back and forth... back and forth, your only job is to notice them, not to judge them, and not to change them.

This can take some practice to get the hang of. But it creates an important separation between the "watcher you" and the "repetitive thought you." The watcher sitting in the chair is the you that has quiet and openness on their side. Without the rumble of ongoing thoughts, you will be a clear channel able to receive intuitive messages. Once you notice your thoughts they are placed on a mental hamster wheel in the back of your mind no longer able to dominate your mental world.

If it is too complicated to visualize your thoughts as they come in then try writing them down for 30 seconds to become aware of your thought patterns.

This meditation helps become more aware of your everyday, monotonous thought patterns. When intuition breaks in to your mind, you will be better prepared to recognize it as not lose it in the thought shuffle!

Clearing Your Body

Have you ever experienced someone saying something to you that was intentionally hurtful? I am sure you have! Think for a moment where you felt that in your body and touch the area where you were feeling the pain. If we are hearing hurtful words and we are processing it in our brain, then why are we feeling it in the body? There must be more going on when we are receiving information.

Your body is a sponge. It absorbs information in the form of energy every day from everywhere you go. This process takes place behind the scenes of our conscious awareness, and usually only draws our attention when the energy becomes overwhelming and transforms into physical pain in our body. These vital energy centers or "chakras" take in environmental data much like our eyes do when we are surveying a room full of people, or a busy highway when we are trying to shift lanes. This energy gathering is a natural function for us as human beings to retain information for the purposes of navigating our relationships with one another and external surroundings.

It is also our built-in security alarm system. When there are dangers or overly negative circumstances our energy will alert our body and mind of potential dangers in the form of pain in the body and fear in the mind. It is essential that we retrain our attention with daily awareness of what our energy is trying to communicate to us.

Unfortunately, we have become a society that pulls all its information from the brain and ignores the messages of the body until the body is in glaring pain.

It is helpful to take an energy inventory every day to access the energy centers, and release any heaviness that has accumulated.

Here is a chakra meditation to check your energy centers and release energy that isn't serving your highest good.

"The Chakra Hotel "

Begin by closing your eyes and seeing yourself standing in the lobby of a beautiful old ornate hotel. You walk up to the detailed brushed copper elevator and push the up button to go to begin your journey. The old doors roll open as you step inside, and rumble gently to a close behind you once you are inside.

You notice that there are 7 floors to this hotel. Each floor represents your energy centers or "chakras." You push floor number one as the elevator begins to lift and take you to your first floor, your "root chakra." The elevator comes to a stop and the doors role open. You cross the threshold into this red root chakra room and take a moment to survey your environment. Is this room small or large? Clean or dirty? Do you feel comfortable in this room? This is the foundation of your energy. After taking in the status of this energy floor, begin to recreate it the way you want it to be. Do you want to rip out the floors and have a stronger surface? Do you want windows or new furniture? This is mentally built and effortless to create. Take a moment to clear this energy room and make it suitable to you. The sky is the limit. Get creative!

After your room is cleaned and updated, walk to the back of the room where you will find a closet. Slowly open the closet and trust what you see. Decided if its contents need to stay or go. Now you are ready to leave this space and return to the elevator and lock the door behind you. Once you are in the elevator you will press the button to the second floor. Next, you will find the orange room represents your sacral chakra. It is responsible for your sensuality, creativity and joy. Again, take note of the status of this room, and begin mentally clearing it out and rebuilding it to suit you. Once you are finished walk to the back of the room and open the closet. Trust what you see and decide if it stays or goes.

After locking the door you return to the elevator and repeat this process for each room. The 3rd floor is the yellow solar plexus chakra room that connects to your personal power. The 4th floor is your green room that connects to your heart chakra, the ability to give and receive love. The 5th floor is your baby blue room and connects to your throat chakra and is responsible for your communication abilities. Speaking and listening. The 6th floor is your indigo room and connects to your intuition and internal visions. The 7th and final floor is your crown chakra. This room is your connection to God and your divine messengers. You have now cleared and reset each one of your energy centers!

Masters of Disguise

The number one question I am asked about Spirit Guide contact is "How can you tell the difference between messages from your guides and your own voice telling you what you want to hear?" This is where the game of trust begins. Everything follows your energy and intention. So, if you are asking for directions from a higher source then you can pretty well bet you have stamped and addressed your message straight to your Guides. The only things left to do are to stay out of your own way and know how to listen for your answers. Spirit Guides are masters of disguise. I have rarely received an answer to a question in the way I expected to receive it. It is usually far more creative and deeper than anything I could ever imagine. They can communicate with you one of two ways. Internally or externally.

How I met Cleopatra from Groupon

Have you ever had a beautiful idea that came back and body slammed you to the ground? Well I did! I thought it would be a wonderful idea to run an ad through a "Groupon" type site for my services to reach more people outside of the metaphysical community. I feel drawn to help people that have never tried connecting to a psychic, so I can hopefully give them a positive alternative experience past the common view of turbans and crystal balls. It is my greatest wish to give the world a chance to see psychics as a talent from God instead of a gypsy side show.

This add ran for one week, and pulled in the masses. It's funny how the world seems so small in concept, but massive when hundreds of people are calling your phone. I hired an assistant to help me navigate the scheduling of so many people. I was booked solid for six months, and I know I met people who I never would have without this ad service. One person that I met stands out the most to this very day.

One day a beautiful African American woman came in for a session. She was dressed in bright silk and had long hair down her back. Her piercing eyes were like nothing I had ever seen before. This woman's energy filled the entire room. Stunned by her radiance, I asked her how she found me and she replied "God sent me."

Struggling to find words, I decided to go ahead and give her my common what to expect when working with a psychic speech. I made it about half way through when she stopped me and said "I do not need the speech, you can go ahead and read me." I closed my eyes and began to tune into this uncharted soul. What I saw threw me for a loop! I was receiving images of Egyptian cats and artifacts along with Cleopatra herself! I hoped this was just a metaphor for some new living room decor she was entertaining but I knew better. I asked her if she was familiar with what a spiritual guide was, and she told me that she absolutely did know of them. I hesitated to tell her what I was seeing when the woman piped in with "I know you're not believing what you're seeing. Just say it anyway."

I can't begin to tell you how difficult it was to trust what I was seeing in this instance. This was turning out to be a personal trust lesson, and little did I know that this was just the tip of the learning curve I was about to encounter. I told the woman that I was seeing a lot of Egyptian symbols around her. Her response was "Yes and.... what else?" I took a deep breath and blurted out "I also see Cleopatra here with you."

The following events took my breath away. It was like an avalanche of wisdom falling on my head with nowhere to run. The woman replied with the unexpected response of, "Now I know you are the real thing, and I can give you the message that God has sent for you."

Paralyzed and confused, I sat still as a statue as the woman continued to speak. "You have no idea how gifted you are, and you have not even yet come close to meeting your full potential. The problem is you're not trusting yourself. Don't throw away your talents!" I quickly rebutted her statement by telling her that I thought I was already doing everything thing I could to trust and expose my talents. Then came another body slam. "You see! You are already not listening! You are failing to trust this message. You need to listen!" I spoke up again telling her that I was receiving the message, I was just confused because I thought she was here for a session and she wasn't allowing me to do my job.

This was the moment I think I officially pushed Cleopatra to her boiling point. "You are still not listening! God pulled me down here to give you a message of your great gifts and you are throwing it away! You are not listening!" The woman stood up and showed herself out of my office as I sat unable to move. I was so stunned by the situation that all I could do was cry. I had never before had someone yell compliments at me. I asked my Guides about the reasoning behind such a bizarre experience. I couldn't understand why this crazy woman was so mad at me for doing my job! Once I calmed down, I could hear my Guides in the form of a thought entering my mind. The thought was "She wasn't crazy."

I decided to call my assistant and vent to her about the unsettling situation, and get her take on this woman when she scheduled her for the appointment. My assistant listened quietly to my rant until I finished, and then broke the news that she had no records of the woman's name I was giving her. She went through all her meticulous notes of the clients she scheduled, still to come up empty handed. No name and no contact number. I decided to contact the Groupon service. They came back with the same answer. No records of the person I was searching for.

The icing on this cake was when I looked up the meaning of the eclectic name my mysterious messenger called herself and the search returned with "karmic law—order within chaos"

Over the years I have thought about that experience more times that I could count. I am grateful now for the messages of awakening my extended gifts that came to me in the flesh. I now know the great lengths that Spirit Guides will go to get our attention. To quote our dear Forrest Gump "Life is like a box of chocolates, you. Never know what you're gonna get!

In case you may be wondering if that was really an incarnation of Cleopatra, I will add that your Guides can most certainly change form at any moment to get their message across. Although, given the amazing events that transpired I still wonder if I was blessed with the opportunity to speak with miss Cleo herself!

Internal Messages

When you are receiving messages internally it can come as "literal" information or "metaphorical." Most of the time the visual and thought messages come through as a metaphor that will need some decoding. Guide messages are layered full of more meaning than what our linear language can convey through words. If you "hear" a mental message, this is most likely going to be a quick few words of wisdom that you can take literally. If you are receiving symbols and signs in meditation or dreams, this is where the decoding fun begins! There is a simple formula to understanding messages from your Spirit Guides.

- First, always ask your Guides if the symbols and images you have been shown are literal or metaphorical.
- If it is metaphor, and your unclear as to what it means, acknowledge what you are being shown and ask for the next layer of the message to be revealed. For example, if you

were to ask your Guides about why you have been carrying extra weight around lately, you may have a thought of an image of a man sitting on a camel. Once you have discerned literal or metaphor, say to your guides "Thank you, I see a man on a camel. What does that mean?"

- Perhaps the next image or thought that comes to you is a glass of water, and you are still not clear about the message. Once again you would say, "Thank you, I see a glass of water. What does that mean?"
- The next thought that pops into your head is a pregnant friend of yours that recently told you that she is retaining water.
- That's when it hits you! Your extra weight is water retention! This may seem like a lengthy process, and one may inquire as to why our guides would not just go to the thought of the pregnant friend.

Believe it or not, most of us don't get it when the answer is right in front of our face! I know if I was shown a pregnant friend in response to a weight gain question, I may panic and draw the wrong conclusion!

You Are the Instrument

Your Guides will often use your personal experiences and knowledge to convey their messages to you. For example, if your Guides wanted to give you the blueprints for a new energy source through a mathematical algorithm you would be hard pressed to receive this information if you did not have a strong math or science foundation for them to bond the information to. If you are an artist and your guides want to send you inspiration for an artistic masterpiece you would be primed and ready to receive it due to your artist background. This is not to say that you couldn't go out tomorrow and gain new foundations in order to draw new intuitive information to yourself. It is just the rule of thumb to remember that your personal knowledge is the antenna that attracts the signal. With every rule or law there comes loop holes and exceptions. It is not uncommon for your Spirit Guides to nudge you to learn and study new areas of interest to upgrade your knowledge base. Often I will have a "hit" to go and Google some strange new topic like ancient Hebrew symbols and without fail in the days to follow I will have a session with someone where that new information was completely necessary.

You are the instrument. A piano can make beautiful music with the right combination of keystrokes. You have the ability to bring through information from the other side as you learn how to tune yourself to the messages of your Guides.

External Messages

When your guides need additional leverage to communicate with you they hit the streets! They orchestrate messages that try and get your attention when the internal messages are not enough to get you moving in the desired direction. They speak through the language of patterns and synchronicity.

Spirit Guides are the masters of well-placed humor and irony. Whenever there is repetitive information that keeps coming back like a boomerang you better believe that it is the handy work of your spiritual surveillance team. It is your Guides job to keep you on track without intercepting your free will. They will often send signs and messages in the form of numbers and animals as well as advice through your friends and family. The universe is a synchronistic system, and life is the beholder of infinite patterns. We find it in all life cycles from plants and animals to eco systems and humans. Our everyday life is full of patterns, swaying most of us to succumb to this repetitious lullaby and become creatures of habit. When non ordinary things occur outside of our normal patterns of life, this is your red flag and universal wake up call.

I remember one day I was torn on a decision whether to go for a work trip in Houston Texas. I was afraid I wouldn't have enough time to squeeze it in before other obligations I had committed to that same month. I was at a complete impasse in my decision. I asked my Guides for feedback on the situation. Only minutes later I was walking through the parking lot of a grocery store when a car came out of nowhere and almost hit me. It scared me, and I felt that the experience was bizarre enough that it must be some sort of sign to get my attention. As the car passed I glanced at the back of it just in time to see that it had Texas licenses plates. Although it was clear to me that this was a message, I wasn't t sure if it was a message to stay or go. Later that evening I was flipping through the television channels and I had a pull that night to check out the History channels. Wouldn't you know that was the evening the history channel was doing a whole series on the Texas Alamo?

I took it as my answer that I should go.

When information repeats itself, and breaks through your normal daily patterns you can begin to feel your Guides speaking and communicating in the external world. These events are wildly referred to as the messages of "non-ordinary events."

Tag Team: Internal and External Messages Unite

On my drive to work one morning my mind was wondering and I began to think about a book that I loaned to a friend that I wish I could get back to re-read. I thought about stopping at the bookstore just up ahead to get another copy but decided against it. A few seconds later my phone began to buzz violently with several text messages from a friend about a celebrity who crashed their car in front of her house. Channel 4 news was trying to investigate the incident and my friend wasn't sure if she should talk to them or not. I took definite note that this was a strange and non-ordinary event. I decided to wait and call her back when I reached my office. My thoughts continued to focus on going to that bookstore. Just as I decided that I wasn't going to stop, a channel 4 news van pulled up right alongside of me in the freeway. I was officially on synchronicity high alert.

Many may think I am crazy, but I don't wait for "third time's a charm." Two channel 4 references was enough to get my attention! I affirmed to my Guides that I felt that I was getting a message, but I wasn't sure what they wanted me to know. I asked for further guidance, and before I could finish my sentence the thought " Go to the book store" entered my mind yet again. I reluctantly turned off the exit to the bookstore, still unclear as to the purpose of my rerouted travel. I noticed that the channel 4 news truck pulled off the same exit I had. I walked into the book store waiting for more information as to my real purpose for being there, when a thought popped into my head "get out a business card." I hoisted my suitcase of a purse on a table and dug until I could find one of my business cards. I decided to walk back to the metaphysical isle, mostly because that's where I always go first. Standing in the isle were two employees. One employee was ensuring the other new employee that she was doing a great job, and instructed her to pull off all of the books called "keys to synchronicity" to reticket. I couldn't help but laugh at the spiritual geek humor and came to the conclusion that this book was the reason my guides pulled me off the freeway. I asked for a copy and the bookstore clerk happily obliged. I turned to leave, feeling like I had reached the end of my message when I heard a voice calling me from behind. "ma'am, I think I know a book you really need to read" I spun around to see the bookstore employee scouring the shelf to find her preferred book for me, a random custumer.

She found the book she was looking for and with a big smile she held it up for me to view. The book was by "The Long Island Medium." She went on to tell me how much she loved this book and asked if I have ever met with a real medium. I am sure my mouth was hanging open as she asked this question. I told the woman that yes, I have. In fact I *was* a psychic medium. She didn't look convinced, and seemed slightly embarrassed. The employee apologized for bringing up the topic of mediums and returned the book to the shelf. No really!! I said. I am a medium…I'm not kidding. The woman looked at me blankly and said "Oh yeah, well then do you have a business card?" My card already in hand, I offered it to her. She looked like she had seen a ghost. The woman began to cry and tell me her personal stories of loss. She was convinced that our meeting each other was heaven sent.

This is still one of my favorite moments of divine synchronicity. Just think. This perfect plan began with channel 4 news. Sometimes the beginning clues are irrelevant to the unfolding circumstances!

Chapter 7

Breadcrumbs to Your Future: Life is A Treasure Hunt

Against the Odds

"Murphy's Law" states that "Anything that can go wrong will go wrong." This is a perfect example of our out grown normal and old broken belief systems. My theory and the promise of your birthright is that sometimes what looks wrong is actually right and anything that is given the opportunity to go right, will go right. Give life half a chance to show you what it is capable of becoming, and it will bloom even against the gravest odds. Life is a beautiful treasure hunt full of boundless opportunities to find your purpose and road to what our soul is searching for. Knowing what we are missing in our life is different, than knowing what we are gaining by living. We may have known our purpose and direction at one time or another in our life but we continue to hold on to versions of yourself that have long since passed.

Human beings are designed to evolve. This isn't a yearly cycle, but a daily one. Your life is a stage for continual reinvention. If you are not having fun or at least getting a kick out of the ironical life processes, than it may be time for a perception shift.

Frequency is everything. "Like attracts like." If, love, happiness, security, and wellness is what you wish to have in your life, then the first step is believing that it is never too late to begin a breeding ground for your desires! Shifting the tides of what you are manifesting in your life is a process, and not necessarily an overnight fix. It took time for you to dig the ditch, it may take a little time to dig your way out. To raise our frequency, we need to focus on more of what we do and much less about what we don't want. Let's prepare now to set off on our first treasure hunt in your life!

The Frequency Jar

Things you will need for your frequency jar:

- an open and reflective mind
- a mason jar (any jar or container will do)
- colorful paper cut up into 4-inch strips (wide and long enough to write a sentence on)
- a pen or marker

Now you are ready to begin!

- Take a few deep breaths and allow your mind to think back on some of your happiest memories. Try not to over analyze, just capture a few snapshots of happy.

- Open your eyes and write the memories that have surfaced each on its own piece of paper and drop it in the jar.
- Close your eyes again and allow your mind to find the times when you felt a miracle that was taking place in your life. Allow as many miracles and memories of unexpected times of relief as you can to come to the surface.
- When you are ready, write down each miraculous moment on a separate strip of paper and drop them in your jar.
- Now, think about the simple and silly things that make you smile. Maybe it's your favorite coffee shop barista or a silly expression your dog or child makes. Look for as many happy life quirks as you can and write them all down on their own strips of paper.
- Finally, think about as many relief activities as you can. Your favorite shows, a special dinner, a walk in the park, a phone call to an inspirational friend, shopping, fun hobbies, or even planning a vacation to look

forward to. Anything that lightens your load. Get creative and dig!

- After you come up with several relief activities, write them down on the strips of paper as well.

Congratulations! You have a great head start on an emergency kit for your energy. Anytime you need a boost, ask your Guides to help you with choosing the right road to recovery and lifting your frequency. Close your eyes and pick out a piece of paper from your jar. This is your breadcrumbs to get you back on top! Keep adding to your jar as you encounter more moments of relief and happiness.

Following the Signs

Recognizing signs and synchronicity is one of the best ways that we can follow the breadcrumbs to our future. Take the time to slowdown and cultivate your trust between you and your guides. When you make the choice to look for signs and follow your intuition, the bond between you and your heavenly team strengthens. In the beginning, I was so afraid I would not recognize my messages that I asked my Guides to show me large signs and hit me with a spiritual 2-by-4 to ensure that I didn't miss them. This helped. My breadcrumbs became loafs of bread placed squarely in the middle of my path, that even on my most distracted day there was no way I would overlook these heaven-sent messages. The best rule of thumb is that if you think you are getting a message from the other side, affirm it and ask your Guides to present the next piece of the puzzle. When you can pick up on the patterns that are around you, the answers to your questions are not far behind. You are becoming a universal code breaker.

Marlee's Sign Story

Marlee was a client of mine in her last year of college. She had worked herself to the bones for the last three and a half years and was on her final stretch of school. She had survived a family crisis, a bad break up and several intense professors. With all of this under her belt she came to me frantic with what she deemed a "complete impasse" in her life.

Marlee was down to the wire and didn't know which topic to choose for a final paper. She felt the topic of this paper needed to be the very definition of her interests in social anthropology. When I asked her why she was putting so much pressure on herself, her honest reply was that she wanted to stand out, and not be like other people. She wanted to write a final paper like no other. Simply put, Marlee wanted to live an uncommon and uncharted life. The instruction I received from my Guides on Marlee's behalf was to give her the tools to find her own answer. I explained to Marlee about watching for signs from her Guides, and how to follow the breadcrumbs. I told her to ask a clear question and to ask for it to be answered within the next few days. To receive the answer, I told her that it was necessary for her to stay extremely present and in the moment for the next few days, and to trust the things that caught her attention.

Marlee came back two days later beaming, with her life treasure hunt experience. She told me that she did exactly as I instructed, except that she asked her Guides to kindly answer her question within the next few hours instead of days, due to her pending deadline. She was a girl on a mission.

Marley explained that she returned to campus after our last session, and as she was walking to her dorm a bird flew right in front of her feet and stayed. She told me that she figured this was her jumping off point, and decided to watch the bird for clues. The bird flew off a few moments later and perched on a garbage can. Marlee followed the bird to the garbage can, and looked inside to see if anything stood out to her. She said the only thing that seemed to be remotely interesting to her in the trash can was a Lancaster's coffee cup.

Marlee decided to go to the coffee shop to see if she could find any messages or clues from her guides. Once in the coffee shop, she noticed a group of kids in the corner, but nothing really stood out. She was about to give up on the treasure hunt, when she heard the kids talking about politics and the school's library. Marlee had the "intuitive hit" that she really needed to follow this through and go to the library. When she made it to the library she found herself stuck once again. Nothing was grabbing her attention. She told me that she closed her eyes and asked to be lead to the "right" aisle. All at once she thought about the kids at the coffee shop and recalled that they were discussing politics.

Although she thought it was a long shot, she decided to go and take a spin around the political section of the library. She walked up and down the aisle, and asked her Guides once again, to show her the next sign. Marlee excitedly explained that a book on one of the nearby shelves was just pulling on her like a magnet. When she removed the book from the shelf, that was when her question was answered. Marlee had found a book misplaced in the political literature section about the "Ancient Pyramids of Giza."

She told me that this experience was life changing, and realized that the push she was feeling wasn't about having the perfect paper, but instead it was about the need to connect with something larger than herself, and connect to a deeper soul relationship with the other side.

Marlee was an avatar when following the bread crumbs! Most of us would never have her patience and determination to trust ourselves to that degree. Although your path of signs may not deliver your answer in three hours or less every time, this story showcases what is possible when you become a co-creator in your life, willing to take a leap of faith and follow the birdie!

Just remember to place your intention to be lead, and sooner rather than later you will find what you are looking for.

Watch Your Speed Limit: Learning to Balance

Balance is key to keeping your energy intact. It is like walking a tight rope when we are trying to keep everything balanced. When life becomes too unbalanced our spirit sends messages to our body and mind to slow down so we can make an assessment of the imbalance and recharge before it sets in to physical weakness.

Our emotions are the home security system within our energetic system. If we are not maintaining our energy or losing energy faster than it can be replenished then irritability, anger, resentment or depression sets in. These if caught early can be reset rather easily. It's when we ignore these ongoing emotional alarms that the energy deprivation can take a more serious toll. As a society, we are under the spell of work hard and run till your empty on the promise of an upcoming weekend or vacation. This is a cycle that is not truly sustainable. Especially the older we get, running on fumes coasts us dearly and our body begins to break down in a more permanent way.

Balancing your energy is a daily practice, one that requires you to slow down and tune in to see if you are close to your max out point. If we have early prevention, we cull stress and strain out of our day and move into power saving mode. Another positive thing that comes from slowing down physically and mentally is that as you slow down physically and mentally your vibration or spiritual frequency raises. Learning to live at half mass allows you to get more done instead of less by working smarter not harder.

Practice slowing down where it is easier and won't affect anything that matters much in the 3D, such as walking to the bathroom slower or taking a few extra moments in the car to breath before you get into work. Try not jumping to respond to your text messages or requests from your family and friends. It's a good rule of thumb to put 5 to 10 extra breaths before you switch any activity. This will allow you to tap back into your higher energy source for a mini refueling session. This importing and exporting of energy is a daily process of balance, and one that will extend your sanity, time, and likely your life. This concept of slowing down to achieve more is a practice used in many cultures around the world for balanced living.

Sometimes we can receive upsetting information or experience something that stresses us out sending us out of balance in a matter of seconds. This type of emotional emergency requires a complete stopping on our part, to safe guard a more serious downward spiral of physical mental and emotional energy loss. No matter if you think you are in a place where that's possible or not, I highly recommend you at least take 10 to 15 minutes to get out of your head and find a place to just breathe and plug in to your recharging station.

In the case of an emergency, try to stay out of the downward spiral and roller coaster of your thoughts. Take your power back immediately and tell the thoughts around the upsetting experience to be silent and take a knee!

Rewind the clock and go back to the last time you felt a full tank of energy and you were in a place of enjoyment. Now hold that memory in your mind and think about the root of that happiness. What was it that allowed you to feel safe enough to enjoy that peaceful, funny or exciting experience. When we are in a state of joy we open the door for an energy recharge through our willingness to receive. When you can't access joy in the moment, go back to the memories and times when you could. Attune yourself through remembering those times when you were able to hold the door wide open and let the light in. Repeat this statement as many times as you need to, **"We are very rarely in actual danger. There is nothing to fear but fear itself. This too shall pass."**

Your brain will tell you in times of upset that this is the be all/end all and the pain that you are currently experiencing may never end. It haunts you with life in prison or the death penalty. When your fear wire gets tripped, take the ropes of your power back as quickly as you can, affirming that you are the one in control. The faster you can get to a place of intervention the better.

If you are experiencing reoccurring stress or anxiety, see if you can pinpoint the pattern. Do you become more stressed and anxious Sunday evening before you were beginning a new work week? Do you find stress invades you in the morning or in the evening? Do your best to find the pattern of your energy dumps. You may find that you have a perpetual bottoming out around certain people, places or situations in your life. Although we can't always change the people or situation that is causing the energy drain we can work to protect our energy before we lose our balance.

Finding that perfect personal prescription for balance does not necessarily mean that you find the answer to all the problems in your life, it simply gives you the tools to keep your days as uncomplicated as much as possible so you can survive in a chaos filled world. The first and hardest thing is just the unlearning of this fast life pace we keep. If you just keep practicing slow pace and energy management to balance you will strengthen your core and eventually become a professional tightrope walker!

A Plan from Sunrise to Sunset Sunrise

I am going to list some energy practices to incorporate into your mornings and evenings to help you on your journey for balance. Sunrise is the promise of a full tank of energy! This is your gift from Heaven and yours to do with as you please. The Tibetan Buddhist have a meditation that has helped through some of the most trying times in my life. It is called the "**Tibetan Death Meditation**." The name may sound ominous, but the practice is beautiful and life changing. The monks begin this simple meditation in the morning where they state "Today, at six o clock I will die." This is not a death wish, but a way to set life in great perspective. It is along the same lines of our western bucket list. If this was your last days, what would be your highest priority. Like the beautiful country song says, "Live like you were dying." There is great peace in simplicity and clarity of focused priorities.

Within the first moments your eyes flutter open to a new day are some of the most powerful seconds to create your masterpiece. Instead of running through your daily to-do list, instead allow your focus to find your highest daily priority. Anything from staying peaceful to cleaning out your refrigerator. Get honest with yourself about the first and most important thing for your upcoming day. Now, ask yourself why it is the most important thing. You may find that the most important thing of your day is the heaviest weighing on you, and the reason behind your choice is to find peace of mind by crossing it off the list. Take a quick moment to visualize the success and highest outcome for you and your priority.

Now you have the Skeleton key to your energy as the day unfolds. You have set the stage, and this sunrise process will dictate the rules of engagement to the rest of your day. This is an excellent exercise for holding your power and focusing your energy. The best part is that you have let go of the potentially anxious scattered mind and any lingering resentment has been brought out of the shadows and is already felt and dealt with! All within just a few morning moments. You are an energy avatar!

Sunset

Now your day is done and winding down, you can see how your agenda played out. It is time to close your day with gratitude. Gratitude for your moments of magic and even the teachers that come in the form of hard knocks.

You have spun your web of energy connecting with different people and places. The time has come for you to clear the canvas for a brand-new slate tomorrow. Begin by tuning in and visualizing any draining energy cords that are emerging from your body and connecting out with the people and places you have encountered throughout the day. This energy attachment happens naturally, and is far from uncommon. It is time to pick up your scissors or sword and cut the cords of energy so they do not continue to drain your energy. Allow your mind to paint the picture of how and where this energy has become attached to you. Pay attention to where the cords are connected. Are they connecting to your heart chakra? Your stomach and solar plexus chakra? Or to the base of your spine, your root chakra? This information will give feedback as to what energy centers are drained the most. Cut all the cords, call on the Angels to help you with this process. Seal this practice with the highest forgiveness your heart can emit. Know that we are all just doing the best we know how to do with the tools that we have. Even your daily offenders most likely reacting from other sources of pain in their life. Forgive them, bless them, and send them on their way. You now have a clean slate ready to for the miracles of tomorrow.

Breaking down the brainwash

Got Ego? I am pretty sure you do. We all do. It's a part of the human formula. The word itself is most commonly used to describe people presenting themselves to be loud and proud inflated with a sense of over importance. To most of us, our own ego feels like a dirty little secret. We put it in our pockets and only bring it out when we are in safe company that is willing to shower it with compliments. The ego is the adhesive to our personality. Without the ego, we would just be a wide-open space with no attachments and no need to be contained.

The actual definition of ego is "A person's sense of self-importance and self-esteem." The ego is just a little thing called our identity and purpose. The ego is best when it can become a part of us in a healthy way by knowing where our gifts and talents lie. On the other hand, when the ego is trying to overcompensate it can create a backwards alter identity with indignation and judgment. The ego can easily be an intuitive blocker. It likes to make the intuitive information bend to its will and make sense on its own terms. I like to call the union of ego and intuition "The Hallmark Channel."

When intuition dances with the ego it can become a made for TV movie that is strung together with your preceptions and emotions, instead informational accuracy. The problem with the ego is that it is the first to fall under the spell of deception. It is the keeper of denial. We see only what we are willing to see within the borders of our identity; we always prefer a story that makes sense to us. To receive clear intuitive guidance the walls of our ego need to fall. To do this we must be willing to be vulnerable and willing to step outside the box of what makes sense. If we step out of our conditioning and mental boundaries, and break the rules of our identity box, what we are left with is infinite possibilities. Information from the other side speaks a language of no beginning and no ending. It is bound only by the limited human capacity to receive it.

I still remember my first lesson in ego and intuition. It was one of the first sessions I had after hanging my shingle as a professional psychic. I had a distressed woman enter my office with bruises on her neck. She wasted no time telling me that her husband was abusive to her and that she wanted to take their two small children and leave him. The woman told me she only had one question for me: should she leave her husband? I felt flushed with anger and judgment, ready to march down to her house, pack up her things and give her a husband a piece of my mind. I have a history growing up with a mother who was a victim of domestic violence. This woman's story hit so close to home. I began to tell her that I would be willing to help her anyway I could. She could even bring her kids to me and I would watch over them so she could go and pack up their belongings.

I started to say all of this in my fight and fury when I had an overwhelming sensation and knowledge from my Guides that she needed to stay with her husband for now. They told me that it was a part of her journey. I became choked with these conflicting emotions. I tried once again to tell her to leave and yet again I was met with a different opinion from the other side. This woman's message was to stay. It took everything I had to tell her that this was the message I was receiving. I even told her that I was probably not getting the right information and she should just follow her gut feeling as to stay or go. The woman became furious with me.

Yelling and telling me that she couldn't take it anymore and that he may even kill her soon if she didn't get out.

I felt terrible for this poor soul. Vulnerable and confused all I could do was tell her once again to follow her gut instincts. The woman left in a fit of tears and anger that I could ever suggest such a thing. I decided that day that I was not cut out to do psychic work and that I should shut down my practice. I couldn't sleep for days worrying about this woman and her small children. I even thought about ways to track her down and help her. I played the situation over again and again, wondering how I could have done something different and heard the "right" message from my Guides.

Two weeks passed when I received a phone call from the woman. She asked if I remembered her and that she wanted to talk to me about the events that proceeded after our session. She told me that she was furious with my message when she left. However, she decided to stay for the time being. The woman went on to tell me that her husband was arrested a few days ago for driving under the influence, and during his time away she could get the help she needed to pack up her and her children and leave once and for all. She told me that her husband was home early and waiting for her the day of our session. In her heart of hearts, she truly believed that had she tried to leave him that day he would have killed her.

My ego had a plan to fight for justice in this experience. What do you do when your ego is telling you one thing and God and your guides are telling you another? Wearing the cloak of indigence and justice we become so immersed with who we are and what we stand for that it can be difficult to see behind the curtain of truth. Life is quite illogical. Thinking about what is fair and right to solve a problem is not always the high road home. Following intuitive guidance doesn't always make sense to your identity story. To breakdown the cycle of the disruptive portion of our ego we must learn to separate the yoke from the egg white and just become the vessel for truth beyond our own limits of thinking.

Think about your triggers, weakness and fears. Begin to access points of your identity where it is hard to see out of the box.

Here is a quick tip on how to separate from the storyteller ego. Before any big decision, or giving other people advice-try imagining a large room with a small glass sound proof room over to the side. See yourself walking into the room and closing the door. You state the intention to be completely out of the way wanting to stay separate from all incoming intuitive information. Before every session, I visualize myself stepping out of the way and into the room, so not to obstruct any of the guidance coming through.

Powerfully Openhearted: A Plan for Living at a Higher Frequency When Good People Go Down

To begin down this brave new path we need to strip down and be willing to let go of old habits and conditioning that no longer serve us. It may not be easy to reset yourself, but it is necessary and worth it. We have not only been carrying our own baggage but baggage for our friends, family, coworkers, and community. This is only the beginning of the excess energy you have been toting around. You are magnetic. Like a human air purifier, collecting energy from everyone and everywhere that needs a good cleaning. Good people collect the most energetic dust. We are the bleeding heart that feels bad when others are in pain. Have you ever said the words "I feel so bad for you"? I know I have!

This is a perfect example to understand what energy is doing behind the stage of our words and good intentions. With this simple statement, we are offering to carry heavy energy to honor the other person who is carrying heavy energy. This is clearly a noble and caring intent behind this suggestion, but there are much better ways to help others that are struggling without putting our energy in jeopardy. We are taught to respond this way, because that is what nice people who care say. Try on this statement for size for someone you love who is in pain, "I will feel good for you."

How does this make you feel? Probably a little awkward, and even downright uncaring. Therefore, we don't deviate from what we were originally taught. If you are thinking that something is simple as a statement can't really affect us all that much, then let me give you the inside scoop on energy transference!

Although you may not completely know just how incredibly powerful you are yet, it is a good beginning to understand the power of your intentions and spoken words. Our words are our will. How we instruct our will is the permission we are giving to what we want to be carried out. Our intention behind our words also plays a part in our transactions. Most of us give birth to good intentions like golden eggs that fail to hatch. This is the nature of being human in the world we live in. We want to help more and do great things but many of these good deeds go undone within the limited hours of our days. Because our energy never dies and only transmutes into other forms of matter, we carry around our good intention golden eggs and the burdens of others until our energy back begins to break.

In the end we wind up carrying more, and giving less.

Giving Energy Away

In my workshops, I often demonstrate how we give our energy away. I hand someone in the class a thousand dollars of Monopoly money and tell them that this is their daily energy allowance. The job of the other class members is to throw out situations and life moments that can happen over the course of a day that drain our energy. Things such as, "McDonalds is backed up in the breakfast line, and it is going to make you late for work," or "Your cat needs an emergency root canal," or "Your car insurance premium went up." Everything from Your best friend wanting you to babysit her house to your spouse being in a bad mood can be an energy dump.

Daily scenarios such as these and many more begin chipping away at your energetic bank balance. We start off strong and feeling rich, almost willing to throw extra energy into whatever crosses our path early in the day and by midday we can feel completely drained. If only we had some energy coupons to cut corners and have enough energy to last the entire day. Here is an amazing fact about your energy. It comes from an endless source. We have access to more energy than we could ever possibly use.

The problem is most of the time we don't tap in to the universal magic well for our boundless energy- we instead spend our "physical energy" from our personal account leaving us feeling drained and tired.

A World of Mirrors: Life Reflects Back at Us.

Each person in your life reflects some part of your soul, even down to the strangers you exchange with on a daily basis. The perfect relationships in your life along with those people who make you want to jump out of your skin are all a part of a grand charade of players that help you to see all aspects of you. When people cross your path, it is like having a hand-written letter from your higher self-requesting that you acknowledge a piece of your personal core. This concept may not be an easy one to digest due to our lifetime experience of seeing everything and everyone separate from ourselves. Many spiritual teachers have said that it is as if we are the projector and our unfolding life is the movie that we are projecting to get a closer look at our multidimensional spirit in many different scenarios and situations.

The story of us is deep and tedious, it is almost impossible for us to know ourselves without our reality bouncing off others. Other people mirror pieces of ourselves back to us to help us see the bigger picture of our energy and emotional creations. It can be helpful at the end of each day to try and notice a pattern or theme of the people that you encountered throughout the day. Did you have a theme of conversations? Are all your friends complaining about their children or husbands? Did you see people laughing and being playful, or being curt and rude?

Like vibrations attract like vibrations and we can continue unwanted cycles if we are unwilling to see our own shadow side or unconscious imbalance. Imagine that you woke up in a wonderful mood and once you left your house you crossed the path of several irritated people who were stuck in a negative view of life. This is probably easy to imagine, because we have all experienced this from time to time. We quickly become frustrated that we had our good mood hijacked and best intentions thwarted by glass half empty people.

Often when we are doing our best to stay at a high frequency we can be shown our shadow sides because we are finally able and willing to see the truth about our subconscious mind. Your shadow side is the part of your personality that you don't generally want to put out for people to view. It is our broken pieces that we sweep under the rug never to see the light of day. When we bury our pain and shortcomings the shadow side of us begins to fester and infect our spirit under the surface. The universal mirror program gives us many opportunities to work through and release the pain and insecurity that binds us and keep us from moving forward as well as affirming where we are on track. When you consider what is being mirrored back, you are not necessarily witnessing your exact circumstances but rather the same root of your subconscious success and struggles—your paraphrased essence.

A simple example of seeing your life in the mirror of other people would be an experience of hearing about a friend or two looking for new jobs because they are unhappy with their current job. This may suggest your own root of unhappiness with your career or your fear of losing a career that you are currently satisfied with. We live in an expansive sea of patterns where everything that shows up in our lives has some meaning even if we can't yet understand the message. Your life is always communicating with you.

The following exercise will help you get to the root of some of your deepest shadows and pain.

The Tri-fold project

One way our intuition speaks to us is through the patterns of our life experiences. If we know what it is we are looking for we can have all the answers we desire about our life just by looking at the events that occur in the day to day. Everything matters. Your life's moments are a messaging system from the other side. Clues and signs are laced through the mundane. You just need to take a step back and focus on the pattern to see the forest instead of the tree.

One night I laid in bed until 2 a.m., tossing and turning writhing in the uncomfortable energy of my anger and hurt feelings. I had an ongoing instant replay of several people in my life that seemed to be a constant drain on my energy. These people never seemed satisfied with what I had to offer, and continually asked for more time and resources than I felt I had to spare.

What hurt the most was their blatant lack of appreciation. Officially disgusted with my mind chatter I decided to get up and do something about this situation. I knew if I could decode and get to the root of this pattern life was showing me I could pull this mind weed once and for all. I sat down at my kitchen table and tore out a piece of paper from a note book and folded in to three sections.

At the top of each section I wrote the name of the person who was causing me this unwanted frustration. I stared down at the three names, and one at a time I wrote a few words about what was bothering me about that person. The first column was dedicated to a friend who I had helped get back on her feet. Each year I would ask the community to help contribute to her family's needs. I would rummage through my own house collecting bags of clothes my children had out grown, duplicate household items and toys I thought the family could use. I would wash all the clothes in hypo allergenic detergent (just in case her children had allergies) fold them neatly, and bubble wrapped the glass dishes. I was more than happy to do it! The problem I ran into with this woman was that she was never happy or thankful for what I would give or do for her. In fact, she never actually said thank you for anything. All that this friend could offer me was a request for "more." I could never fill her bucket of need.

I wrote down under her name everything I could think of that was causing me pain in this relationship. Ungrateful, unsatisfied, energetic drain, never says thank you, unappeasable, guilting, and more.

Another friend was chosen for the second column who had just moved close to me from another state. Upon the first month of her arrival I took her out to lunch multiple times and drove her around the city so that she could get her bearings and learn how to better navigate her new surroundings. This friend was excited to be in a new city and eagerly wanted me to show her all of what this corner of the world had to offer. She continued to ask for favors and advice and much like my other friend, no "thank you" or words of appreciation was sent my way. I again, wrote on the paper under her name all the qualities that were the source of my frustration and hurt.

Finally, the last column bared the name of a family member who I had been trying to help through a life crisis. I would spend hours on the phone listening to her stories of life disappointments and painful moments. I bought and gave her books to help her rediscover herself. Only again to find the same pattern that it was never enough for her and she remained dissatisfied with my help.

I continued to write down all my grievances with all three women. Next, my guides instructed me to find what all the women had in common. I quickly found that it all boiled down to evidence of people who were ungrateful and quick to take advantage of my kindness. This was mirroring back to me the essence of ingratitude. I was incredibly perplexed by this finding because I felt like I was an extremely grateful person.

My Guides nudged me to go deeper to solve this mystery. I knew that these situations had to be some important information speaking to an imbalance I was struggling with deep inside of my spirit. I meditated for several minutes when I had an epiphany and this answer brought all my loose ends together. I realized that I was creating my own pile of resentment by continually over extending myself and dumping out all my energy reserves when no one was asking for my help. I was peddling my good will and wants for these women when I had not once been asked. I was trying to kill them with kindness because I didn't think I could hold a friendship without being an over the top extraordinary human.

The universal mirrors showed me my flawed thinking as I was exposing my savior addiction. This is a perfect example of how good intentions can cover up our self-worth and keeps us from experiencing the feelings of deeper understanding of pure unattached giving. I have used this trifold process several times throughout my life and it has always succeeded in explaining how people are mirroring my own soul back to me.

Chapter 8:

Bonni's Top 10 Breadcrumbs for Life

1. Emotions are not the Enemy

Emotions are not the enemy. They are mood messages from your spirit that help inform you about your balance settings. Without emotion, we would not have our much-needed interventions. Don't shoot the messenger! Sometimes we are hanging onto life by a thread—feeling stressed out, overwhelmed and angry at the crosses we must bear. When emotions tap on the door to show us the way back home to peace and sanity, we open the door and then we slam it shut, telling it to get off our property and that we are not buying anything from them today. This emotional messenger is the life shift that you have been asking for. It comes to break down the patterns of chaos. It is hard to think of pain being a positive thing but honestly, we learn to open to the idea of change when we are at some of our most unhappy places. Just remember to hold and wait for the next step to be revealed. Don't wait for the whole picture to be explained to you, just ask for the single next step for your soul to take. The journey begins with the first step.

2. Mental Dandelions

Your thoughts are just like dandelion seeds that blow in the wind. They are dispersed immediately after birth as they catch the wind to find a patch of ground to root and begin to grow. Each thought seed follows the same process whether it is a desirable though or a fear of something you don't like or want in your life. It creates whatever you have initiated. Taking your life back means learning to be aware as much as possible about what you are thinking. Negativity begets more negativity as positivity breeds more positivity with the seeds of thought that you release. Try to slow down and take an inventory of your thoughts several times a day. Changing your life begins from the inside out as you birth your thoughts into a positive creation. You are a powerful soul, and just like a genie in a bottle the Universe will response to your calls from the subconscious. Don't wait for happiness to find you. Create it! Stop, Drop and Love.

3. Become a co-creator in your life

A wait and see attitude should come only after you have created the foundation to set things in motion. If you don't set the stage of your life someone else will try and set it for you. If you ask God or your Guides what you should be doing in your life, you will often receive the response "What do you want to do with your life?" This is not a puppet show. You are supported in exposing your soul in all that it is craving to express. This is a journey of seeking and uncovering the core of who you really are. If we were just told what to do all the time we would miss out on the heart of life. We are here to express ourselves and to be guided within our own choosing.

All over the world in every culture you will find ritual and ceremonies. This is because intention and action create sacred movement and miracles. When you set an intention it is a super-powered thought that begins the ball rolling for creation. When you add an action to your desire, this solidifies your intent further into your reality. Blessing your food before you eat is an example of setting an intention followed by an action. Setting the intention of commitment with the action of giving a ring, making a wish and blowing out birthday candles or writing a letter to someone who has hurt you and then burning it in a fire are all common experiences of setting intent followed by the seal of an action. Your life is sacred. Every moment matters. When you are co-creating in your life with your spiritual advisors you are honoring life with focused living with a cause and a purpose. Intent and action help you to deepen your connection to all of life and create from a space of honor and love.

4. Love Larger

We all can get stuck in the details of our life and forget about our place in a larger arena in our Earthly community. We have good intentions and sometimes struggle to follow it up with action. We fall into the belief that we are only affecting the small group of people around us and that our individual life is the biggest picture. We turn on the news channel and feel defeated as the stories of unrest only grow in numbers. It is too much to hold onto the bigger picture. After all, we are just one person and can't see how one person could clean up such a big worldly mess. The answer is to love larger than ourselves. We set forward a radical "pay it forward" movement that becomes infectious and far reaching. Love has no limit to family or community, it can expand across the entire planet and beyond if you just remember to set the intention. It is hard to believe we are that capable but we absolutely are. When we love larger we not only create a ripple effect of light in others, we become full of light within the process of giving.

Here is an exercise to begin loving larger.

Find your nearest Walmart (any large store will do) and set the intention before you enter the building to expand your ball of light and energy into a sphere larger than the whole building. Focus your love and set the focus to shine your light as bright as the sun. Enter the building carrying this radiant light and just make a loop around the store. What you will begin notice is that people are holding their gaze on you, and even sending a random smile your way. There is a profound shift that will take place. Practice lifting the frequency of everyone in the store, and feeling the true power of loving large. Hold your light until you exit the building. Give a sealing intention that all that who were touched by your light pay it forward to others the rest of the day. In a matter of minutes, you can create miracles, move mountains, and love hundreds of people into a life of higher living. Gandhi understood this larger love when he told us to "Be the change we wish to see in the world "

5. Back to Basics

Your personal energy can be powerful yet still fragile. Balancing your self is a full-time job. The key to preventing an energetic imbalance is slowing down and checking in with yourself to ensure that what you are receiving is equal or greater than what you are giving. We cannot go for long on an empty spiritual tank before we start to tap into our physical energy creating an imbalance. When you take a moment to assess your energy take that time to pause and refuel your resources. This only takes a minute, and can truly have a make it or break it difference. To check out and checkup first, slow your daily pace or even come to a complete stop. Feel your feet rooting into the ground and visualize the top of your head and the center of your heart opening like a blossoming flower. See the pure God light: the essence of love pouring down from the heavens into your head and heart. You can even receive this light through the palms of your hands. Take deep breaths as you allow your energy to be refueled. Say the words "Let it go" to release anything heavy holding you down. Once you feel complete, see the light form a protective sphere around your body to keep your mind and spirit in balance. Set the intention of your life perspective. Be clear on how you want to proceed through the rest of your day.

If you come to the point of feeling completely overwhelmed, remember to just get back to the basics. Cut out all the excessive static around you by coming back to setting simple priorities for the day. Try not to over extend yourself creating more of an energetic imbalance. Cut your life activities in half and return to the core of who you are to reset your system. You will find balance by returning to your natural home and God connection. Just keep it simple.

6. Recess for your mind

Remember, you are not the same person you were five years ago, nor are you yet the person you will become. We can become lost in translation as our evolving spirit tries to fit into last season's thinking. Our mind must grow with our spiritual journey, or we become fragmented and loose our purpose of soul. In the movie" Runaway Bride," the mother of the runaway bride asks her daughter after her latest runaway why she is unable to make the commitment of marriage. Her daughter tells her mother about losing herself in relationships. She uses the analogy of eggs. With one man, she ate poached eggs because he liked them, another man she only ate scrambled, and another relationship after that only eggs over easy. The bride said to her mother that she was tired of running, and needed to take time to find her own eggs. This can be true for many of us as we get swept up in the needs and wants of others, and who we use to be.

Check in with yourself once a week updating your mind to better serve your intuition. Let go of the things that you cannot change and focus on your own next steps. Allow your mind to experience the reality of your expanding spirit through regular meditation. When you allow yourself the opportunity to slow down in meditation it is like having a mental recess. Can you imagine how different school would have been without breaks and recess? Your adult mind still needs this time to open to your ever-changing spirit and fly free.

7. Use it or Lose it

The reason our intuition has become muted or altogether lost is that the older we became the more we stopped flexing our intuitive muscles. Most of us believed that imagination is just child's play. We became disconnected from the magic in the mundane and became serious analysis driven adults. Imagination is our connection to what lies beyond our world; it is the gateway into all that is outside of the backyard of our brain. You can't think yourself to the other side, you must believe and open the portal of your imagination to recover this lost art of communication. Opening the door to your intuition takes time. You are lifting the years of calcification from yourself and retraining pathways in the brain reaching beyond its borders. Children are our teachers, they are tuned in and tuned up as they march to the beat of their own drum and care less about social graces. Tapping into the intuitive realm begins with feeling safe within your creative side. If you feel that you have lost touch with creativity this is most likely your intuitive block. Try sitting with your family or friends and telling a fictional story. Start with a main character and circumstances you create and pass it to the next person to add to the story. Keep passing it back and forth until you practically have an award-winning screen play. Becoming the Storyteller is a fast way to reconnecting to your creative mind setting the stage for your intuition switches to be turned on. Let your inner child rise to the surface and become one of your best spiritual teachers.

8. Listening to Heaven's CEOs

Spirit Guides are your greatest assets in life. Knowledge that you are never alone, and always have guidance to turn to helps you focus on the flying while releasing the worries about falling. Guides are contracted to help you navigate the storm; not to take away the rain. The storms are valuable lessons that will help shape us from the inside out drawing out the fabric of our faith in something greater than ourselves. Our job is just to remember to ask for the help and be ready and willing to receive the messages. Life is a treasure hunt. Your Guides are trying to communicate with you 24 hours a day. Keep your eyes peeled and watch the synchronistic breadcrumbs lead you to the next step on your unfolding journey. Trust yourself, if it feels like a sign it is a sign. If you don't understand the message your Guides are delivering, affirm what your receiving and ask for more information.

9. Grounding with Gratitude

Gratitude is the receiving energy and is also a practical way to ground and invoke stillness. When you focus on what you are grateful for you bring your energy into the present moment. When in the present moment you have greater alignment with mind body and spirit allowing creative forces to run through you to manifest your dreams into reality. Gratitude is one of the most powerful tools in your tool box to heal yourself and your life. It is almost impossible to feel our worldly worries and be imbalance when we are immersed in deep gratitude. Deep gratitude is different than just knowing what you "should" be grateful for. This type of radical gratitude runs down into the caverns of your spirit moving you closer to God and the sacred nature of all things. This profound practice creates something that we are all endlessly searching for: peace.

10. You are the White Crow

Rise above and embrace your unique authentic self. You are a leader on this planet and have the opportunity to become a lighthouse for the dark sea around you. Remember that you came to Earth with a purpose. This above all is the most important part of our soul evolution. We are moving into the other side of normal where there is a revolution on the horizon calling you to develop yourself and become stronger within the intuitive realms. If you have felt different all your life this is an individual indicator that your gifts were meant to shine now, at this time on the planet. The world needs your intuitive insight and willingness to live powerfully openhearted. Gather your spiritual resources and practice unyielding balance so that you can take your place and be willing to stand in your truth and power. Your "different" is your talent. Be willing to stand up for your intuition and live as a white crow, proud of your unique beautiful spirit.

Everything Matters

One of the greatest things I have learned working with people and being in the business of explaining life forecasts, is that every piece of the puzzle counts, down to the last drop!

Every thought and thing did not come from nowhere, it all came from somewhere. Matter is in the form of things, and things are born from thought. Everything matters. Your life and the whole world surrounding it is a tapestry of meaningful experiences. If we take a step back, we can see that the whole living world is just a series of patterns in the spiral of life. Even down to the leaves on a plant, or petals on a flower, it is just grand flawless patterns. There isn't room for accidents in this orderly creation, all is relevant down to the most mundane moments. The larger than life equation represents universal perfection even if we can't see the whole big picture. With everything holding a purpose in life this means that we have countless opportunities to build a relationship with our soul. If something is crossing your path, no matter what it is, it has purpose and is speaking to you. Absolutely everything matters, from the street signs you pass to the strangers you meet. These are messages from your life trying to have a conversation with you.

Once you have the ability to see that everything truly is connected events don't seem to just happen to you anymore. You take on the role as director rather than the actor. To begin learning this life language the first thing you need to consider is that life is the container for everything sacred. We begin by living life as if each moment is a gift and dialogue with God. This first step is the most complicated task for some people. It seems too cumbersome to take in all moments as special. This practice is a cultivated art. The art of living at a higher frequency requires you to set your dials to seek the magic in the mundane. Miracles are not designed for a special occasion, they are present within each hour of the day.

How to Spot the Magic in The Mundane

We need to experience life like a child. Children are the masters of finding magic in the mundane. They can find humor in something as simple as an insect, gratitude in the form of an ice cream cone, and a miracle in the depths of a sandbox. This transformation doesn't happen overnight, but it doesn't take long to embrace the theory of hourly miracles! This isn't a message to just cut loose and get carefree. This is an active participatory league of life force you are joining. One that will teach you how to experience life through the veil. Come to the light side, and I will show you how to become a permanent resident!

Start today by putting on your new goggles and begin to see your life through the eyes of a child. You may have to fake it until you make it, but I promise this practice will be life changing if you can just stick with it for a few days. Three days can rock your world and shift your perception if you just put in the effort and intent.

Try going outside and hunt down the nearest insect and watch the way it moves and the way it interacts with your energy. Spend an hour taste testing all 31 flavors of ice cream. Find the mystery that lies within the "birthday cake" flavor. Try talking to someone you don't know and get deeper that a smile and a "how are you." Strike up a conversation with the checkout clerk at the grocery store, and really listen to what they are saying. This may seem silly, but the more you let your "freak flag fly" the quicker you can make the shift into a miracle seeker! Seeing as a child sees helps you to tune into the subtle intuitive world. This is the where you are able to hear, see, feel, and know what is under the surface layers—finding the magic in the mundane.

I created a program a number of years ago with children and adults, where we conducted a role reversal revival. The children were the teachers and the adults were the students. The process was that the adults would ask sincere questions in a childproof manner about their largest life hang ups, and inquire about how they should handle their stress. The children presented the adults with advice and a plan on how to find happiness. For this to make a real difference each of my adult had to at least promise that they would attempt to carry out the advice of their child mentor. The adults would ask things such as "How can I get some sleep at night I am so stressed?" or "How can I hold my temper?" and "How do I get a better job?" There is no question in my mind that God, Angels, and Guides work through children. Their answers were simple, but filled with so much revelation that it would send shivers up your spine. Some of the children's antidotes were to forgive their parents, spend time with trees, paint bright pictures on their office walls, play with a dog, smell the rain, drive fast when no one is looking, eat cheesecake. Out of the mouths of babes were messages to heal our lives.

The Number 19

I once had two lovely young ladies come to me seeking intuitive training. After the very first session they were highly excited to start their journey to an intuitive driven lifestyle, and ready to take the first assignments home and put them to the test! I explained to them about Spirit Guides and how they operate in everyday life. For homework, I asked the women to implore their guides to send them a personal sign, so that they would know how to develop a trusted question and answer relationship. I wanted the women also to see how we can receive messages from beyond that were not just happenstance. I explained that some of the most common ways we receive messages from our Guides was in the form of numbers, through the practice of numerology. Numbers can be traced back to patterns, and those patterns can give way to paragraphs of written meaning and messages. I also shared with the women to be on the lookout for any repetitive animal signs, as animals are also living patterns of information your guides can easily manipulate and send information through.

The woman promised to ask their guides for guidance, and be on the lookout for answers in the form of synchronicity.

Here is the magic and miracle that they found hidden in the mundane!

The women were both beside themselves with excitement when they returned a week later for the next session. They couldn't wait to share the experience they both had encountered. The first woman told me that she had asked for her guides to send the answer to a question about her life's direction in the form of a number. She asked to receive this number and coordinating message at a rare time when she least expected, so it would be clear that it was a sign from her Guide. The woman explained that nothing was happening with a response to her question until one night she agreed to watch her friend's 2-year-old little boy while the friend had a Saturday night out on the town.

As my client was bathing the little boy and getting him ready for bed, out of blue the boy started yelling "19! 19! 19!" again and again without prompt or reason. The woman was sure that this was the sign she had been waiting for! I was just about to comment on what an amazing experience this was, when I was told that there was more to the story and that it had not yet reached the craziest part! The other young woman began to tell me her Guide story. She said that the same evening around the same time she too received the answer to her question. The woman said that she was driving behind a fire truck when all at once she got the "hit" or knowing that the number of that fire truck was going to be the answer from her Guides. When she looked down at the unit number, it read number 19. The next day the two women spoke, and were blown away to find that the same evening they both had been given the numerical message of 19.

This is a great example to show how we can receive answers to our life questions in the form of signs. One woman was given the answer to her questions audibly and the other woman had a hit of just knowing her answer had arrived.

If we are not prepared and willing to seek the magical undercurrent of life, many of our answers and signs can become lost in translation.

Take the number and animal challenge! Ask your guides a specific question and ask them to answer you in the form of a number or animal.

Be willing to follow these three guidelines.

- Ask your question and be patient.
- Seek out your answers in the form of magic in the mundane.
- Believe it when you see it! Trust yourself if you get a "hit" or knowing about

the answer. Trust anything that stands out as a non-ordinary event.

The Real Magic Word: Gratitude

The Gratitude Challenge

I always considered myself a very grateful person. My "thank- yous" came out like a cannon ball shot from a cannon: intense and repetitive. I wondered why the more times I would thank someone the quieter they would become. It was a very strange phenomenon. I could feel that my thank- yous were not getting in. Gratitude is a receiving energy and it is important to cultivate a strong foundation within it to become better at receiving intuitive information. I came to realize that receiving wasn't easy for most people and my gratitude was bouncing back like pebbles on the widow of a one-sided star-crossed lover. I took on the quest of finding a better way to be able to receive. I was lead to the practice of a" Radical Gratitude Challenge."

It is a process of giving only under the circumstances of truly feeling grateful. In the past when I would offer up an incessant stream of thank yous it was coming from a place of guilt. I felt bad that anyone would be put out by my requests or lifestyle. I also found myself apologizing with almost every sentence no matter what the topic was. I was addicted to needing everything and everyone to be ok before I would be ok. This is a codependent lifestyle that is built on the foundation of shame and guilt. It was impossible to receive with any depth, because I was drowning in a sea of shame. Why you might ask? Most empaths are accustomed to managing the energy around them. They don't do conflict, and will run around the room checking in with everyone until they feel it is safe from any potential discord. Empathic people already feel everything around them and they tend to block any additional receiving, in fear they will become consumed and overwhelmed by energy. This is a vicious cycle. This problem with this process is that you end up blocking the good with the bad.

I acknowledged this hamster wheel I was on and dedicated myself to really feeling head to toe gratitude before I would deliver it to its destination. I woke up every morning for 14 days, to sit for several minutes in a state of gratitude. This was not a laundry list of topical suggestions of where I was thankful in my life, but an all over consuming feeling from my head to my toes and in every cell of my being of feeling gratitude. Some days I could only feel this deep feeling for one or two things in my life. I was looking to find quality gratitude over quantity gratitude. I felt I owed God and the universe the sincerest appreciation I could muster up for the gifts that were bestowed in my life.

It turns out that the universe loves a truly grateful heart! I noticed that my life started unfolding like a well-oiled machine. Anything I wanted to happen that day seemed to roll out like a red carpet. My thank-yous were so heartfelt that when I planted them on unsuspecting strangers, friends, and loved ones they would instantly stop and receive willingly, instead of looking awkward and shutting down. People can feel the intent and root behind your words. I have no doubt that what I was emoting before my gratitude shift, was shame and pain. No wonder they didn't want my thank- yous! This energy of deep gratitude can bring people to the depths of humility where there is the most powerful experience of life one could ever ask for.

Radical Gratitude is contagious. If you can move into this place, you become a wide-open recipient of the Christ Consciousness. You begin to radiate light and love. I can see now why I couldn't receive earlier in my life. I did not feel worthy enough to accept this much love, or any love for that matter. Shame will sell you short and make you believe that you only deserve second hand light and love. It closes the door for your capacity to receive communication with the other side. If you are stuck on a shame setting, acknowledged it, and ask your Guides and Angels to remove this weight from your heart.

The "Radical Gratitude Challenge" is simple!

- This is a 2 week commitment to sit in silence a few minutes each day and find the things that you are most grateful for in your life.
- Pick one or two of those things and sit with them, breathing deeply with your hands on your heart.
- Breathe into the place of gratitude until your body begins to tremble, tingle, ache or vibrate with the sensation of deep gratitude.
- Don't give up if you don't get this right away. The feelings will come if you just keep setting your intention.
- This momentous feeling will stay with you throughout the day attracting more of the same feelings of gratitude.
- Try to give your gratitude throughout the day only after you really can feel it.

- After 2 weeks you will find that you embody gratitude more often and will begin see and feel the miracles in your life unfold as you live as a full-time resident of universal flow.

The Power of a Moment: "Be still and know that I am God"

Hold onto your seats! As we travel through interstellar living and investigate how "time" holds us back and "space" accelerates our movement forward to our intuitive life and evolving spiritual understanding. To get a glimpse of this human plight, imagine that time is just a strand of silk, and space represents the pearls on this silk strand. Time has the function of holding space. The way we experience space in our reality, is in the form of a moment. Believe it or not, a moment in time is your daily opportunity to gain multidimensional soul knowledge.

The Information Age has a broken speedometer. Our current societal standard is "the faster that you go the better you will be." Our modern motto is "Get it before it's gone," and if you're not fast enough, you will be left behind or worse... run over! We can find ourselves driven by impulse to supersize our schedule and top load any found free time with tasks, in the hopes that we can get everything done, feel accomplished, and collapse into a moment of relaxation at the end of the day. Even I find myself falling hook line and sinker for this speed fest some days.

Hard work and focus goes into time being saved instead of spent, and can ultimately be working against you on your spiritual journey. The flaw in this system is that time is one dimensional and not designed for any type of depth. Although we stack our goals to the ceiling sealed with our timeline, ultimately time is not the best container for our dreams and ambitions.

Somewhere we became mixed up, and our value of space has been diminished. Anything that is memorable to us can be found within our life moments. At the end of each day when someone asks us how our work day went, we respond with an accounting of significant moments. Sometimes we recall a series of moments that added up resulting in a bad day. Other times we have only joy and excitement to share. The golden opportunity that we are missing out on is our willingness to slow down time as we journey deeper into the space of a bottomless moment.

Here is an example of how time and space can play different roles in our life. Think about a time when a friend or coworker gave you a birthday card full of beautiful messages. You opened the card, smiled, and for a few seconds you were deeply touched by this gesture. You hugged your coworker or friend and told them how grateful you were. This whole interaction took place in just a minute or two and added to a positive moment in your daily bucket. This is a very moving experience as it is, but imagine if you opened the card, read the beautiful words, and sat in the moment with the emotion of deep gratitude and joy as it continued to expand for five minutes. Now picture your friend or coworker standing by and silently waiting as you spent time going deeper into the moment. In this day and age pulling a stunt like that would be social suicide and land you with a reputation of being chemically imbalanced.

However, what would be gained is priceless as you accept the opportunity to meet pieces of yourself that you didn't even know existed. Diving deeper into the space of a moment is like traveling through a wormhole to the very core of your soul. You would expand simply by exceeding your own limitations and breaking these topical layers of your everyday reality. Five minutes in return for a greater understanding of self that can last a lifetime.

It is time for a prison break! Our spiritual growth and sanity depends on it. It is our primary job to reclaim our powerful moments and standup to the time bully! The good news is that there is a way to hold, and go deep within a moment without becoming socially outcast. Our emotions are the gateway to this deep human space. They are the wind beneath our wings and fuel that drives us. Even though we prefer emotions that make us feel good, all our emotions are worthy tools.

The Power Moment Challenge

Set your intention at the beginning of your day to be alerted at the first opportunity of a significant emotion. This emotion can be happy, sad, angry, grateful, joyous, repelled, or even frightened. Any emotion will do the trick for your power moment challenge. As you continue this practice, you can seek out a variety of different emotions to experience the hologram that is your soul. Once you have captured a significant emotion, ask yourself to stay open and feel the emotion even deeper. Pay attention to what this space draws to your surface. Remember, your main job is just to hold the door open and relaxed deeper into the moment. Stay clear of any expectations, just surf the emotional wave. Eventually you will find the eye of the storm where there is simple stillness. This is the space within the moment where you can ask your life questions, and hear a divine response.

Notice the alchemy process of beginning with one emotion and surfacing with a new variation and range of feelings.

Our ultimate goal is to reach the parts of ourselves that can't be accessed through the surfaces of our daily life. Instead of waiting for our emotional knowledge to blow up in our face like a volcano, God has given us the ability to regularly access our own internal compass. We have been given the gift of pearls, and it will take us all the way home to a place of fulfillment and personal peace.

The Midas Touch: Creating More of What You Want

Several years ago, I was training a gifted channel and medium when she brought through a very interesting message about the law of attraction. Her guides asked her to share the theory of women and their obsessions with anti-wrinkle face cream. The message was stating that women spent great amounts of energy and focus on how to look younger. They rigorously seek out new creams and ointments to make their wrinkles disappear. The problem with this was that so much of their intent was spent going in the wrong direction to obtain what they wanted most.

Women are placing all their energy on what they didn't want instead of what they did want. If they could just put as much emphasis into their soft supple skin, as they did their wrinkles the ageless look would be theirs to keep. In a nut shell, we were being told that our human train goes a hundred miles an hour to the wrong destination.

This really stuck out for me. I remembered when I went to school to become a hypnotherapist one of the first things that they taught us was to speak the language of the subconscious. They gave us the example of someone who wanted to quit smoking. If you are trying to help someone quit smoking under hypnosis, you should not use the words "not" or "won't." Everything you said had to be spoken in the affirmative. The subconscious mind could not relate to anything that was based in lack. Instead of hearing "You will not smoke" the subconscious mind would hear "You will smoke." We were taught to always speak in the affirmative, with language suggesting forward motion. "You are now a non-smoker."

If you think of our human subconscious as just a smaller version of larger universal consciousness then they must both operate by the same standards, just a different scale. This would explain why our thoughts can be responsible for much of what is unwanted in our life.

With science predicting that 85 percent of our thoughts are negative, it is easy to see how manifesting what we want in our lives needs to be a conscious focused attempt, and not something left to chance within our internal default settings.

This concept of manifesting what you want in life took root in my heart. I decided that I would dedicate my meditation practices to receiving insight as to how we can reverse the effects of chronic negative thinking. Over time, I received so much information, that I had enough to put together workshops and clinics on this topic. I thoroughly enjoyed teaching these classes but I couldn't dismiss the number one question that continued to be asked and I couldn't yet answer.

"If time isn't really what we think it is, then why does it take such a long time for you to manifest what you want in your life? Is instant manifestation possible?" This question haunted my curious need to know mind.

I would lay awake thinking of all the stories of historical alchemist, and even Jesus who turned water into wine, and promised us that we could do all that he could do.

How can we manifest what we want instantaneously? I couldn't find any answer that suggested that we couldn't or one that ensured that we could. I was stuck.

The Unknown Blessings of a Snoring Husband

One night around 2 a.m., I awoke to the sound of snoring. My poor congested husband was raising the roof with this loud and unpleasant sound. I was ready to start shaking him awake as any loving wife who valued her sleep would do, when I had a rogue thought enter my head. "What if you could stop the snoring without even laying a finger on your deep sleeping husband?" I could feel that my Guides were up to something so I paused to hear what they had to say. I had the immediate understanding that this was the answer to instant manifestation that I had been waiting for. I could practically hear word for word my Guides talking to me, as I was being instructed through these next steps.

I sat up in bed and was told that if I wanted to stop the snoring, then I needed to get focused and clear on what it was I really wanted in that moment. I decided that my true desire was silence. I was told to hold that focus as I inhaled and gathered the silence. I decided to take this literally, so I began leaning back and forth scooping up the silent air from my husband in between his loud snores. I would pause when he would begin to make noise, and return to my collection process as he would fall silent once again. I absolutely trust this divine guidance but I would be lying if I told you I didn't feel completely ridiculous as I sat collecting air much like rowing an invisible boat. Then again, I bet Tesla, Columbus, and Einstein doubted their sanity from time to time as they teetered on the threshold of the possible and impossible.

Twelve minutes had passed as I continued to gather my silence. I felt a calm come over me and a sense of neutrality to the sounds that had originally annoyed me. I was impressed with this process and felt I could fall back asleep easily unaffected by the loud snoring. Before my head returned to the pillow, I had another full body feeling that there was more still to be learned as a student of the other side. I closed my eyes, and could hear in my mind as the second half of this experiment was unfolding. I was instructed to take all that I had harvest and to now enhance my exhale while releasing the silence back into the space of silence. I simultaneously stretched out this invisible substance, as if I were pulling apart hot salt water taffy.

Having nothing to lose, I began exhaling my breath targeting this silence like a heat seeking missile sending it back to its original home. I stretched the elastic air as wide as my arms could reach for several minutes. My findings were not that of instant change, but the experience left me close enough to feel the effects of alchemy. The sounds of snoring slowed and became much less frequent, growing quieter over the course of the following moments until the only sound left was a heavy breathing. I couldn't help but wonder if this was just a lucky coincidence, or if I truly effected change over the course of 20 min. I decided to take this theory to the streets, and practice on other life annoyances.

I tried it in many different experiments, everything from my misbehaving cat to lack of sunshine on a cloudy day. I harvested all the things I did love and stored them until a rainy day. I began to believe in this formula more and more, feeling like I stumbled across the meaning of life. I took this theory to the very root of humanity to seek out the thing that we all crave the most in life. My conclusion was love. Feeling inflated and grateful to have the answers for all of mankind I was higher than life lifted in my knowledge that all we need is love. All at once another thought hit me upside the head and brought me back to Earth.

The Beatles solved this mystery 40 years earlier.

"All We Need Is Love" is not my original discovery.

I had to laugh at myself. The facts that I now know to be true about manifestation is as follows:

1. To get more of what you want you need to focus on what you "do" want, not what you don't want.

2. You need to hold this focus while seeing where remnants of the thing you want is already present in your life.

3. You need to first get to a place of neutrality, and find radical gratitude for life as it is.

4. Finally, keep asking for what you want, believing it will come, and not needing it in the present moment to be happy.

How to Bring Light into Dark Places

When you are in a dark place in your life, everything you do feels like you are fighting just to stay afloat. You doubt yourself around every turn and each moment feels like you have swallowed bricks and they are collecting in your chest and stomach. The voices of your fears are direct and confidant informing you that a wrecking ball is coming your way. These life experiences are the dark night of the soul and although you attempt to pull yourself out nothing seems to have a permanent fix to your heavy heart. When you are being assaulted with heavy emotions you must "get bold." We feel in our dark spaces that we have lost our light and our power.

Getting loud and proud is the way you begin the boomerang process for your energy. If it is fear and anxiety you are in battle with tell the voice of fear to be silent! Say it like you mean it! You are in the driver's seat, tell your fears to go to the back and sit down while you decide where your destination is. No matter if it is fear, depression or anger that has got ahold of you, the first step is always to take the reins back and regain some evidence of your power. Get louder than whatever is haunting you. The next step is to determine if the emotional energy that you are carrying is yours or someone else's that you have been babysitting.

Ask your Guides if the energy you are feeling and carrying is "yours or someone else's." Next, get out of the way and trust the answer you hear in your mind. If the heavy emotional energy belongs to someone else, then call in your Spirit Guides and Angels to cut all cords of this negative energy and send it to where it belongs. Close your eyes and think about breathing the white light of Heaven in through the top of your head and exhaling and heaviness or negativity. You are quite literally drawing light into dark places. Before long you will begin to experience a gradual shift of energy returning you back to your original state. This is rarely immediate. You need to refill your energy tank, and this may take a few hours or in some cases even days. If the response you receive from your Guides is that the energy is yours, the next step is learning how to hold in the heavy.

Learning How to Hold in the Heavy

Holding still at any time isn't always our favorite thing to do, much less when you're in a state of fear, anxiety or anger. Learning to hold in the moments of heavy emotion means that you are no longer furthering any story line that wants to stick to your thoughts like glue. You are just sitting with the emotions wordlessly. If you are successful at quieting your hamster wheel story telling then you clear the stage for your Guides to give you some insight to help you better understand the pain you are carrying. When you have the answers to why, the how to fix it falls shortly behind. In some cases, once you understand what is ailing you the heaviness leaves almost instantaneously.

Knowledge and deep insight is the anti-venom for our fears. When you are holding in the moment you are just acknowledging how you feel without an escape plan. This is strength training for the soul. Scientists believe an emotion only lasts 90 seconds, anything after that we are just recycling the story in our mind and resetting the same emotions.

When you are holding in the heavy you are separating yourself as the experiencer and the receiver. This feels like you are in a novel about your life as you simultaneously experience moments in first and third person. Once you notice that you are experiencing undesirable emotions and hold the door open to receive, the emotional beast begins to lose its hold over you because you no longer believe its story.

Holding Heavy with My Soup

One beautiful day I decided to spend my off day being a domestic goddess. This day was that type of day when you clean your whole house and feel destined to take the cleaning renegade overboard to the organization all junk drawers. Just before my kids were scheduled to get off the bus I had finished the cleaning and decided to top it all off by whipping up a tasty soup. As I was stirring my soup a heavy irritation overcame me. My first thought was that this emotion of irritation quickly turning into anger was strange given the wonderful day I was having. I decided to nip it before it grew any larger and ask my Guides if this was "my" energy or "someone else's." I immediately received the messages of "this is all yours." I knew to keep the door open and receive more insight on the troublesome energy while holding in the experience.

My mind kept trying to wander off and find a story for the situation "Why are my kids so messy? "I always have to spend any free moments cleaning up after them!" and "I am so sick and tired of no one seeing how much effort I put into making this house a clean and loving home. I'm just the maid in the background!" I continued the efforts of pulling my thoughts away from the storytelling and back to holding my silent emotional station. My children came through the front door like soldiers returning from war. They slung their heavy backpacks on the couch and made a trail of socks and shoes all the way to their bedrooms.

My emotional holding battle increased to maximum capacity. The stories were becoming louder as they mocked me for trying so hard to keep a clean house, confirming that I was in fact invisible and just a glorified house keeper. You may think that this was an over exaggerated series of thoughts and feelings, because after all kids will be kids, it's not personal it is just the checked-out minds of adolescents. You would be absolutely right in your opinion of this simple everyday situation. In these instances of inflammatory emotions all stories are high and mighty. You will notice emotions will attach to story lines using words such as "always "and "never" coming from a place of indignant judgment. This is the nature of the beast.

I continued to hold and breath deeper stirring my soup with my growing anger when all at once I had an out of the blue word pop in to my mind "calendar." I knew this was my Guides trying to break in to my congested energy even though the statement "calendar" didn't mean much to me. I decided to just walk over to the calendar in my kitchen. I stared at it for a few seconds and the next thought that entered my mind was "Wow, I had no idea it was already the 17th. I thought to myself "That's funny I should be staring my menstruation cycle today." Followed by the epiphany that my hormones were the cause of my random spike of anger and irritation. The cloud of emotional discomfort broke instantly and I felt a return of my happiness.

Just as soon as I understood the why behind the emotion all my loud stories lost their voice and purpose. If I had not chosen to hold in this situation, it would have been easy to place this energy on my children yelling at them for their laziness, apathy and disregard for their hard-working mother. I have no doubts that if I decided to stir the family pot instead of the soup, the virus of irritability would have spread throughout the house affecting my entire family. Holding your heavy instead of instant reactions will always serve you. In the end, you may receive information from your Guides instructing you to council your lazy children, but you will have learned to hold the door open and receive. This life skill will help you to keep your energy intact using intuition over angry analysis for the highest outcome.

Although I have had many situations where I have held the door open in the face of intense emotions, this experience goes to show just how much knowledge truly can be the prescription for your happiness.

The Long Haul: Your Intuitive Aftercare Plan – Thriving on the Other side of Normal

The other side of normal welcomes you as its newest resident. The intuitive lifestyle shifts you are embracing are hard work in the beginning, but the effects it will have in your everyday life are priceless. I know in my heart of hearts that intuition is our birthright. We were sent here with greater guidance to achieve our spiritual destiny and to know that we are loved beyond measure. The first rule of maintaining your connection to higher living is to never stop chasing inspiration. To be inspired is to be full of higher spirit.

Choosing spirit over the material and intuition over logic is a daily discipline. As you walk the balance beam of life you will fall off more times that you can count. You will forget to ask when you need guidance the most, and fall for your fear's trickster stories. You will lose your balance and dump all your energy into a moment of guilt. You will feel silly about following intuitive signs and doubt your messages. You will have days where all you can do is complain about what you don't want instead of what you do want. You will even have days when you can't be still, even for a single moment. All of this and more will still sneak its way into your new normal but the miracle occurs within your willingness to return to the road of intuitive mastery.

The decision to walk on higher ground and honor your soul by seeking the magic in the mundane and building foundation for inspiration is the light at the end of any dark tunnel. The more you practice taking leaps of faith the more you will see beyond the threshold of the veil to the other side. Life is a test of faith and intuition is all about believing beyond what you understand and have always known. Thriving on the other side of normal means allowing yourself to become an untethered soul by loving without walls and trusting the inside more than the outside. To be guided you must allow yourself to be lead. To be lead you must have the ability to listen for the direction. To hear the direction you must be able to hear the still small voices behind the loud words and trust yourself as the receiver.

Close each day with deep gratitude, and begin each day with a sincere intention. Everything that falls between will soon become the life you have been waiting for. Imagination and appreciation are your tools for the long haul. Choosing to believe beyond is an act of courage. The brain doesn't always like or understand your choice to bypass its conclusion of reality. Human beings have historically feared what they do not understand and cannot see with their eyes.

Above all, you are walking the path of an enlightened warrior. A soul with a calling to seek inspiration and a determination to see your mission through to the very end. Your intuitive abilities will peak as you follow the breadcrumbs and stay focused on the next steps of your spiritual schedule. When you least expect it your fear with give way to strength, your doubts will fuel the fire of renewed inspiration- and intuition will feel like simple thinking.

The heart is becoming the new brain as we adjust to hold the bigger picture and unlock the catalyst for these long overdue changes. When we can truly trust and love ourselves it is easy to see what we have been missing and what we want most in our lives. Our future takes on a whole new face when we see that we are not in this life space alone and blindfolded. We begin to see evidence of love in everything and understand that to change your life you must first be willing to receive the gift of the impossible turning into the possible. Gratitude is nothing more than falling in love with your life over and over again. Your heart is the voice of your spirit and the recipient of intuitive communication from the other side.

The more we practice powerful openhearted living the more inspiration and epiphany becomes a part of our everyday encounters with God. In this new intuitive age we will still have our battles with fear and regret. The moment we truly believe that everything matters equally and that we are always guided will be the moment that we will have learned to fly and forgotten how to fall.

About the Author

Learning to fly means forgetting how to fall.

This is the personal life mantra of internationally successful psychic, Bonni McCliss. At the tender age of four Bonni began her relationship with spiritual beings. By the time she was a young adult she was diagnosed psychic.

Imagine being at rock bottom, in an endless place of dark with no comfort, then one day someone comes and throws the curtains open letting in the forgotten beauty of light. That was when Bonni turned her head up and spread her wings.

Bonni now uses her unique gift to help individuals better understand their lives, by sharing the detailed information from divine messengers. We all have guides and Bonni instructs others to reach their highest potential and achieve their dreams through the life-changing messages she receives.

Praise and loyalty flow from the diverse international clientele Bonni serves that includes many celebrities and historically significant properties. She is widely known as a down-to-earth, inspirational messenger with extraordinary abilities and proven accuracy.

A mother, wife, leader, community activist, nature lover, entrepreneur and

Certified Hypnotherapist, Bonni and her family live with their many animal companions in a quaint community in Tennessee.

When not appearing on television, writing, conducting retreats and workshops or doing readings, Bonni is available for speaking engagements. To find out more or book Bonni for your event, workshop, or readings go to www.psychicbonni.com

Made in United States
Orlando, FL
29 September 2023